Resist Much, Obey Little

RESIST MUCH,

Edited by
James Hepworth and
Gregory McNamee

OBEY LITTLE

Some Notes on Edward Abbey

HARBINGER HOUSE
Tucson, Arizona

Harbinger House, Inc.
Tucson, Arizona

Manufactured in the United States of America.

This book was set in 11/14 Bembo.

Library of Congress Cataloging in Publication Data

Resist much, obey little : some notes on Edward Abbey / edited by James
    Hepworth and Gregory McNamee.
        p.   cm.
    Bibliography: p.
    ISBN 0-943173-45-0 : $10.95
    1. Abbey, Edward, 1927–1989—Criticism and interpretation.   2. Abbey,
Edward, 1927–1989—Interviews.   3. Authors, American—20th century—
Interviews.   4. West (U.S.) in literature.   I. Hepworth, James, 1948–
II. McNamee, Gregory.
PS3551.B2Z85   1989   813'.54—dc20   89-15461

Contents

Preface to the Reissue

In Memoriam Edward Abbey, 1927–1989

Edward Abbey, to crib a well-known line from Walt Whitman, contained multitudes. He was a deeply generous man, one of the most generous we have ever known: he was absolutely unsparing of his time, his money, his intelligence, himself. He thrived on thunderous arguments, and, although God knows he could be gruff, he was never discourteous in waging them. He inspired and influenced generations of writers, artists, ecologists, and desert rats, as the contributors to this book attest; almost everyone doing creative work in the American West today owes Ed a debt. He was always sharing some discovery or another, some new novel or painting or essay or mountain trail. He loved good cigars, difficult books of twentieth-century continental philosophy, discussions that went on late into the evening, slow country tunes back-to-back with selections from Brahms and Mozart or from the composer whom he called his hero, Charles Ives. He was fond of thick, grilled, bloody steaks, although he hated the corrupt ranching industry that thrives, subsidized by the American taxpayer, on our public lands. He despised fakery, cowardice, the usual pieties. He applauded deliberation, honorable action, the unfettered mind. He held little sacred, and he vigorously tested the convictions of his friends and opponents alike, probing, questioning, arguing. When he died, on the fourteenth of March, 1989, he left a hole in our hearts, in the heart of the American West, in the heart of modern American writing.

Whatever Ed did, he did with rare good humor, even in the thick of combat; for that reason, he had few real enemies, no matter how controversial the positions he took. When we went together for the first time to Jack's, a now-defunct, chic bar in the heart of downtown Tucson, Ed set the theme by walking through the swinging doors and bellowing, "Smells like lawyers in here!" It was a safe enough accusation, since attorneys are thicker than cockroaches in the booming West; every carefully coiffeured head in the place turned. Ed smiled cordially, flashed that big, toothy, utterly charming grin of his, whereupon all but the most self-important of his targets laughed and settled down to argue politics until closing time. Try Ed's humor for yourself: go out and buy a copy of his novel, *The Fool's Progress* (Henry Holt & Co., 1988), published six months before his death to widespread acclaim.

Ed contained multitudes, and he will be remembered in as many ways as there are people who came to know him. One of our favorite reminiscences of Ed comes from a grade-school composition by a young girl named Brady Barnes that Ed showed us one spring day a few years ago. Brady's perceptive, funny account—bearing all the promise of a true writer—delighted him, as he took real joy in so many good and noble things:

FAMOUS STAR EDWARD ABBEY
Edward is a writer. He writes about how to blowup
dams. The name of one of the books he wrote was
called *Monkey wrench gang*. He wears a black hat with
a wrench on it. Ed has a gray elephant beard and he's a
tall, skinny man. Ed does not like the highway so he
throws beer bottles out the window. Ed does not like
t.v. so he took his t.v. outside and took his gun and
shot his t.v. and now it's a sculpture in his backyard.
by Brady.

For our parts, how shall we remember Ed Abbey? First of
all, let us continue to read him, to keep him alive by return-
ing often to his words. Let us hold *Desert Solitaire* and *The
Journey Home* and *Black Sun* and Ed's other books close to
our hearts, recommend them often to others, read them
aloud in lines at the Motor Vehicle Division and the neighborhood Safeway, talk about them, buy them so that they
stay in print forever. And then, let us continue the struggle
to keep something of the real America alive, to preserve the
wilderness, to demand ecological responsibility, to fight for
the Earth without compromise: let us act with the courage
that Ed taught us, for he remains among us, a part of the
good fight.

Finally, borrowing again from Walt Whitman, let us remember Ed Abbey by honoring a favorite credo:

Resist much, obey little.

Introduction

Edward Abbey has been busy, over the last twenty-five or so years, making not one but several reputations for himself. He is now nationally known, of course, as a writer of novels, essays, and magazine pieces, and he has come far enough in his craft that even *The New York Times Book Review* takes notice when a new Abbey book appears. *The Monkey Wrench Gang* pops up in conversation in Boston and Chicago; *Desert Solitaire* sells across the land; and Abbey's work as a whole enjoys a respectable circulation. Abbey is also well known, in the environmentalist community, as a defender of the land, a radical preservationist, a staunch opponent of the boomers, developers, and hustlers who infest our nation in seemingly endless numbers. In the American West, too, Abbey has gained a reputation for other kinds of political activism, owing to his having taken controversial stands on such issues as feminism, immigration, even first-run movies.

In any event, Abbey's name has gotten around, although not always for the right reasons. To the young, the college-aged, Abbey has been presented as something of a guru, the monkey wrench as mystical mantra (see the introduction to "The Poetry Center Interview," in this volume, for an example of the pop-star treatment). To Western conservatives, his views are dangerously left-wing; to liberals, his opinions carry dreaded overtones of self-sufficiency, "elitism," and other bugaboos. And to Arizona journalists, lacking a hot subject since Richard Kleindienst went underground, he is simply good copy, an inexhaustible fund of controversy and "human interest."

Readers seeking any such treatment here will, we are pleased to say, be disappointed. Our concern here has been to engage in a bit of honest, simple, non-academic criticism, not of a guru or a crank, but of an artist and his work. The task set on our contributors has been to free Abbey from the various camps that claim him and to discuss him unadorned. Thus we have Wendell Berry, William Eastlake, and Barry Lopez telling us why Abbey *matters*, why we should bother to take account of him at all; we have Richard Shelton, Nancy Mairs, and Robert Houston, among others, pointing out significant aspects of Abbey's work; we have Gary Snyder and Sam Hamill girding up for a round or two of ideological wrestling; and, through selected interviews, we have Abbey himself, making his own case and thereby complementing—and sometimes correcting—the interpretations of others. What has emerged, we hope, is a competent and well-rounded rendering of Abbey and the various facets of his life and thought that brought him to the public's attention in the first place.

We are grateful to Tom Auer and Marilyn Auer, the editors of *The Bloomsbury Review*, for their many acts of kindness, including their permission to reprint Dave Solheim and Rob Levin's interview with Abbey, which first appeared in their pages; to Carson Productions, Ltd., for their kind permission to publish Charmaine Balian's interview with Abbey; and to Tanya, Cheyenne, and Melissa for their encouragement and help.

James Hepworth
Gregory McNamee

Resist Much, Obey Little

Wendell Berry

A Few Words in Favor of Edward Abbey

Reading through a sizeable gathering of reviews of Edward Abbey's books, as I have lately done, one becomes increasingly aware of the extent to which this writer is seen as a problem by people who are, or who think they are, on his side. The problem, evidently, is that he will not stay in line. No sooner has a label been stuck to his back by a somewhat hesitant well-wisher than he runs beneath a low limb and scrapes it off. To the consternation of the "committed" reviewer, he is not a conservationist or an environmentalist or a boxable ist of any other kind; he keeps on showing up as Edward Abbey, a horse of another color, and one that requires care to appreciate.

He is a problem, apparently, even to some of his defenders, who have an uncontrollable itch to apologize for him: "Well, he did *say* that. But we mustn't take him altogether seriously. He is only trying to shock us into paying attention." Don't we all remember, from our freshman English class, how important it is to get the reader's attention?

I

Some environmentalist reviewers see Mr. Abbey as a direct threat to their cause. They see him as embarrassingly prejudiced or radical or unruly. Not a typical review, but representative of a certain kind of feeling about Edward Abbey, was Dennis Drabelle's attack on *Down the River* in *The Nation* of May 1, 1982. Mr. Drabelle accuses Mr. Abbey of elitism, iconoclasm, arrogance, and xenophobia; he finds that Mr. Abbey's "immense popularity among environmentalists is puzzling"; and observes that "many of his attitudes give aid and comfort to the enemies of conservation."

Edward Abbey, of course, is a mortal requiring criticism, and I would not attempt to argue otherwise. He undoubtedly has some of the faults he has been accused of having, and maybe some others that have not been discovered yet. What I *would* argue is that attacks on him such as that of Mr. Drabelle are based on misreading, and that the misreading is based on the assumption that Mr. Abbey is both a lesser man and a lesser writer than he is in fact.

Mr. Drabelle and others like him assume that Mr. Abbey is an environmentalist—hence, that they, as other environmentalists, have a right to expect him to perform as their tool. They further assume that, if he does not so perform, they have a proprietary right to complain. They would like, in effect, to brand him an outcast and an enemy of their movement, and to enforce their judgment against him by warning people away from his books. Why should environmentalists want to read a writer whose immense popularity among them is puzzling?

Such assumptions, I think, rest on yet another that is more important and more needful of attention: the assumption that our environmental problems are the result of bad policies, bad political decisions, and that, therefore, our salvation lies in winning unbelievers to the right political side.

If all those assumptions were true, then I suppose that the objections of Mr. Drabelle would be sustainable: Mr. Abbey's obstreperous traits would be as unsuitable in him as in any other political lobbyist. Those assumptions, however, are false.

Mr. Abbey is not an environmentalist. He is, certainly, a defender of some things that environmentalists defend, but he does not write merely in defense of what we call "the environment." Our environmental problems, moreover, are not, at root, political; they are cultural. As Edward Abbey knows and has been telling us, our country is not being destroyed by bad politics; it is being destroyed by a bad way of life. Bad politics is merely another result. To see that the problem is far more than political is to return to reality, and a look at reality permits us to see, for example, what Mr. Abbey's alleged xenophobia amounts to.

The instance of xenophobia cited by Mr. Drabelle occurs on page seventeen of *Down the River*, where Mr. Abbey proposes that our Mexican border should be closed to immigration. If we permit unlimited immigration, he says, before long "the social, political, economic life of the United States will be reduced to the level of life in Juarez, Guadalajara, Mexico City, San Salvador, Haiti, India. To a common peneplain of overcrowding, squalor, misery, oppression, torture, and hate."

That is certainly not a liberal statement. It expresses "contempt for other societies," just as Mr. Drabelle says it does. It is, moreover, a fine example of the exuberantly opinionated Abbey sentence that raises the hackles of readers like Mr. Drabelle—as it is probably intended to do. But before we dismiss it for its tone of "churlish hauteur," we had better ask if there is any truth in it.

And there is some truth in it. As the context plainly shows, this sentence is saying something just as critical of ourselves as of the other countries mentioned. Whatever the justice of the "contempt for other societies," the contempt for the society of the United States, which is made explicit in the next paragraph, is fearfully just: "We are slaves in the sense that we depend for our daily survival upon an expand-or-expire agro-industrial empire—a crackpot machine—that the specialists cannot comprehend and the managers cannot manage. Which is, furthermore, devouring world resources at an exponential rate. We are, most of us, dependent employees."—A statement that is daily verified by the daily news. And its truth exposes the ruthless paradox of Mexican immigration: Mexicans cross the border because our way of life is extravagant; we have no place for them, or won't for very long. A generous immigration policy would be contradicted by our fundamentally ungenerous way of life. Mr. Abbey assumes that, before talking about generosity, we must talk about carrying capacity, and he is correct. The ability to be generous is finally limited by the availability of supplies.

The next question, then, must be: If he is going to write about immigration, why doesn't he do it in a sober, informed, logical manner? The answer, I am afraid, will not suit some advocates of sobriety, information, and logic: He *can* write in a sober, informed, logical manner—if he *wants* to. And why does he sometimes not want to? Because it is not in his character to want to all the time. With Mr. Abbey character is given, or it takes, a certain precedence, and that precedence makes him a writer and a man of a different kind, and probably a better kind, than the practitioner of mere sobriety, information and logic.

In classifying Mr. Abbey as an environmentalist, Mr. Drabelle is implicitly requiring him to be sober, informed, and logical. And there is nothing illogical about Mr. Drabelle's discomfort when his call for an environmentalist was answered by a man of character, somewhat unruly, who apparently did not know that an environmentalist was expected. That, I think, is Mr. Abbey's problem with many of his detractors. He is advertised as an environmentalist. They *want* him to be an environmentalist. And who shows up but this *character*, who writes beautifully some of the time, who argues some of the time with great eloquence and power, but who some of the time offers opinions that appear to be only his own uncertified prejudices, and who some of the time, and even in the midst of serious discussion, makes *jokes*.

If Mr. Abbey is not an environmentalist, what is he? He is, I think, at least in the essays, an autobiographer. He may be writing on one or another of what are now called environmental issues, but he remains Edward Abbey, speaking as and for himself, fighting, literally, for dear life. This is important, for if he is writing as an autobiographer, he *cannot* be writing as an environmentalist—or as a special ist of any other kind. As an autobiographer, his work is self-defense. As a conservationist, he is working to conserve himself as a human being. But this is self-defense and self-conservation of the largest and noblest kind, for Mr. Abbey understands that to defend and conserve oneself as a human being in the fullest, truest sense, one must defend and conserve many others and much else. What would be the hope of being personally whole in a dismembered society, or personally healthy in a land scalped, scraped, eroded, and poisoned, or personally free in a land entirely controlled by the

5

government, or personally enlightened in an age illuminated only by TV? Edward Abbey is fighting on a much broader front than that of any "movement." He is fighting for the survival, not only of nature, but of *human* nature, of culture, as only our heritage of works and hopes can define it. He is, in short, a traditionalist—as he has said himself, expecting, perhaps, not to be believed.

Here the example of Thoreau becomes pertinent. My essay may seem on the verge of becoming very conventional now, for one of the strongest of contemporary conventions is that of comparing every writer who has been as far out of the house as the mailbox to Thoreau. But I do not intend to say that Mr. Abbey writes like Thoreau, for I do not think he does, but only that their cases are similar. Thoreau has been adopted by the American environmental movement as a figurehead; he is customarily quoted and invoked as if he were in some simple way a forerunner of environmentalism. This is possible, obviously, only because Thoreau has been dead since 1862. Thoreau was an environmentalist in exactly the same sense that Edward Abbey is: he was for some things that environmentalists are for. And in his own time he was just as much an embarrassment to movements, just as uncongenial to the group spirit, as Edward Abbey is, and for the same reasons: he was working as an autobiographer, and his great effort was to conserve himself as a human being in the best and fullest sense. As a political activist, he was a poor excuse. What was the political value of his forlorn, solitary taxpayer's revolt against the Mexican War? What was politic about his defense of John Brown, or his insistence that abolitionists should free the *wage* slaves of Massachusetts? Who could trust the diplomacy of a man who would pray:

> Great God, I ask thee for no other pelf
> Than that I may not disappoint myself:
>
> And next in value, which thy kindness lends,
> That I may greatly disappoint my friends . . . ?

The point, evidently, is that if we want the human enterprise to be defended, we must reconcile ourselves to the likelihood that it can be defended only by human beings. This, of course, entails an enormous job of criticism: an endless judging and sorting of the qualities of human beings and of their contributions to the human enterprise. But the size and urgency of this job of criticism should warn us to be extremely wary of specializing the grounds of judgment. To judge a book by Edward Abbey by the standard of the immediate political aims of the environmentalist movement is not only grossly unfair to Mr. Abbey, but is a serious disservice to the movement itself.

The trouble, then, with Mr. Abbey—a trouble, I confess, that I am disposed to like—is that he speaks insistently as himself. In any piece of his, we are apt to have to deal with all of him, caprices and prejudices included. He does not simply submit to our criticism, as does any author who publishes, but virtually demands it. And so his defenders, it seems to me, are obliged to take him seriously, to assume that he generally means what he says, and, instead of apologizing for him, to acknowledge that he is not always right or always fair. He is *not*, of course. Who is? For me, part of the experience of reading him has always been, at certain points, that of arguing with him.

My defense of him begins with the fact that I want him to argue with, as I want to argue with Thoreau, another writer full of cranky opinions and strong feelings. If we value

these men and their work, we are compelled to acknowledge that such writers are not made by tailoring to the
requirements, and trimming to the tastes, of any and all.
They submit to standards raised, though not made, by
themselves. We, with our standards, must take them as they
come, defend ourselves against them if we can, agree with
them if we must. If we want to avail ourselves of the considerable usefulness and the considerable pleasure of Edward
Abbey, we will have to like him as he is. If we cannot like
him as he is, then we will have to ignore him, if we can. My
own notion is that he is going to become harder to ignore,
and for good reasons—not the least being that the military-
industrial state is working as hard as it can to prove him right.

It seems virtually certain that no reader can read much of
Mr. Abbey without finding some insult to something that
he or she approves of. Mr. Abbey is very hard, for instance,
on "movements"—the more solemn and sacred they are,
the more they tempt his ridicule. He is a great irreverencer
of sacred cows. There is, I believe, not one sacred cow of
the sizeable herd still on the range that he has left ungoosed.
He makes his rounds as unerringly as the local artificial
inseminator. This is one of his leitmotifs. He gets around
to them all. These are glancing blows, mainly, delivered on
the run, with a weapon no more lethal than his middle finger.
The following is a fairly typical example:

> The essays in *Down the River* are meant to serve as anti-
> dotes to despair. Despair leads to boredom, electronic
> games, computer hacking, poetry and other bad habits.

That example is appropriate here because it passingly gooses
one of my own sacred cows: poetry. I am inclined to be
tickled rather than bothered by Mr. Abbey's way with

consecrated bovines, and this instance does not stop me long. I do pause, nevertheless, to think that *I*, anyhow, would not equate poetry with electronic pastimes. But if one is proposing to take Mr. Abbey seriously, one finally must stop and deal with such matters. Am I, then, a defender of "poetry"? The answer, inevitably, is no; I am a defender of some poems. Any human product or activity that humans defend as a category becomes, by that fact, a sacred cow—in need, by the same fact, of an occasional goosing, an activity, therefore, that arguably serves the public good.

Some instances of this are funnier than others, and readers will certainly disagree as to the funniness of any given instance. But whatever one's opinion, in particular or in general, of Mr. Abbey's blasphemies against sacred cows, one should be wary of the assumption that they are merely humorous, or (as has been suggested) merely "image-making" stunts calculated to sell articles to magazines. They are, I think, gestures or reflexes of his independence—his refusal to speak as a spokesman or a property of any group or movement, however righteous. This keeps the real dimension and gravity of our problem visible to him, and keeps him from falling for easy answers. You never hear Mr. Abbey proposing that the fulfillment of this or that public program, or the achievement of the aims of this or that movement, or the "liberation" of this or that group will save us. The absence, in him, of such propositions is one of his qualities, and it is a welcome relief.

The funniest and the best of these assaults are the several that are launched head-on against the most exalted of all the modern sacred cows: the self. Mr. Abbey's most endearing virtue as an autobiographer is his ability to stand aside from himself, and recount his most outrageous and self-embarrassing goof-ups, with a bemused and gleeful

9

curiosity, as if they were the accomplishments, not merely of somebody else, but of an altogether different kind of creature. I envy him that. It is, of course, a high accomplishment. How absurd we humans, in fact, are! How misapplied is our self-admiration—as we can readily see by observing other self-admiring humans! How richly just and healthful is self-ridicule! And yet how few of us are capable of it. I certainly do find it hard. My own goof-ups seem to me to have received merciless publicity when my wife has found out about them.

Because he is so humorous and unflinching an autobiographer, he knows better than to be uncritical about anything human. That is why he holds sacred cows in no reverence. And it is at least partly why his reverence for nature is authentic; he does not go to nature to seek himself or flatter himself, or speak of nature in order to display his sensitivity. He is understandably reluctant to reveal himself as a religious man, but the fact occasionally appears plainly enough: "it seems clear at last that our love for the natural world— Nature—is the only means by which we can requite God's obvious love for it."

The richest brief example of Abbey humor that I remember is his epigram on "gun control" in his essay, "The Right to Arms." "If guns are outlawed," he says, "only the government will have guns." That sentence, of course, is a parody of the "gun lobby" bumpersticker: "If guns are outlawed, only outlaws will have guns." It seems at first only another example of sacred cow goosing—howbeit an unusually clever one, for it gooses both sacred cows involved in this conflict: the idea that, because guns are used in murders, they should be "controlled" by the government, and the idea that the Second Amendment to the Bill of Rights confers a liberty that is merely personal. Mr. Abbey's sentence, masquerading as an instance of his well-known "iconoclasm," slices cleanly through the distractions of the controversy to the historical and constitutional roots of the issue. The sentence is, in fact, an excellent gloss on the word "militia" in the Second Amendment. And so what might appear at first to be merely an "iconoclastic" joke at the expense of two public factions becomes, on examination, the expression of a respectable political fear and an honorable political philosophy, a statement that the authors of our constitution would have recognized and welcomed. The epigram is thus a product of wit of the highest order, richer than the excellent little essay that contains it.

Humor, in Mr. Abbey's work, is a function of his outrage, and is therefore always answering to necessity. Without his humor, his outrage would be intolerable—as, without his outrage, his humor would often be shallow or self-exploitive. The indispensable work of his humor, as I see it, is that it keeps bringing the whole man into the job of work. Often, the humor is not so much a property of the argument at hand as it is a property of the stance from which the argument issues.

Mr. Abbey writes as a man who has taken a stand. He is an *interested* writer. This exposes him to the charge of being prejudiced, and prejudiced he certainly is. He is prejudiced against tyranny over both humanity and nature. He is prejudiced in favor of democracy and freedom. He is prejudiced in favor of an equitable and settled domestic life. He is prejudiced in favor of the wild creatures and their wild habitats. He is prejudiced in favor of charitable relations between humanity and nature. He has other prejudices too, but I believe that those are the main ones. All of his prejudices, major and minor, identify him as he is, not as any reader would have him be. Because he speaks as himself, he does not represent any group, but he stands for all of us.

He is, I think, one of the great defenders of the idea of property. His novel *Fire on the Mountain* is a moving, eloquent statement on behalf of the personal proprietorship of land—*proper* property. And this espousal of the cause of the private landowners, the small farmers and small ranchers, is evident throughout his work. But his advocacy of that kind of property is balanced by his advocacy of another kind: public property, not as "government land," but as wild land, wild property, which, belonging to nobody, belongs to everybody, including the wild creatures native to it. He understands better than anyone I know the likelihood that one kind of property is not safe without the other. He understands, that is, the natural enmity between tyranny and wilderness. "Robin Hood, not King Arthur," he says, "is the real hero of English legend."

You cannot lose your land and remain free; if you keep your land, you cannot be enslaved. That is an old feeling that began to work its way toward public principle in our country at about the time of the Stamp Act. Mr. Abbey inherits it fully. He understands it both consciously and instinctively. It is this and not nature love, I think, that is the real motive of his outrage. His great fear is the fear of dispossession.

But his interest is not just in *landed* property. His enterprise is the defense of all that properly belongs to us, including all those thoughts and works and hopes that we inherit from our culture. His work abounds in anti-intellectual jokes—he is not going to run with *that* pack, either—but no one can read him attentively without realizing that he has read well and widely. His love for Bach is virtually a theme of his work. His outrage often vents itself in outrageousness, and yet it is the outrage of a cultivated man—that is why it is valuable to us, and why it is interesting.

He is a cultivated man. And he is a splendid writer. Readers who allow themselves to be distracted by his jokes at their or our or his own expense cheat themselves out of a treasure. The xenophobic remark that so angers Mr. Drabelle, for example, occurs in an essay, "Down the River with Henry Thoreau," which is an excellent piece of writing— entertaining, funny some of the time, aboundingly alive and alert, variously interesting, diversely instructive. The river is the Green, in Utah; the occasion is a boat trip by Mr. Abbey and five of his friends in November, 1980. During the trip he read *Walden* for the first time since his school days. This subjection of a human product to "the prehuman sanity of the desert" is characteristic of Mr. Abbey's work, the result of one of his soundest instincts. His account of the trip is, at once, a travelogue, a descriptive catalogue of natural sights and wonders, and a literary essay. It is an essay in the pure, literal sense: a trial. Mr. Abbey tries himself against Thoreau and Thoreau against himself; he tries himself and Thoreau against the river; he tries himself and Thoreau and the river against modern times, and vice versa. The essay looks almost capriciously informal; only a highly accomplished and knowledgeable writer would have been capable of it. It is, among all else, a fine literary essay—such a reading of *Walden* as Thoreau would have wanted, not by the faceless automaton of current academic "scholarship," but by a man outdoors, whose character is in every sentence he writes.

I don't know that that essay, good as it is, is outstanding among the many that Mr. Abbey has written. I chose to speak of it because Mr. Drabelle chose to speak of it, and because I think it represents its author well enough. It exhibits one of his paramount virtues as a writer, a virtue paramount in every writer who has it: he is always interesting. I have read, I believe, all of his books except one, and I do not remember being bored by any of them. One reason for this is the great speed and activity of his pages; a page of his, picked at random, is likely, I believe, to have an unusual number of changes of subject, and cover an unusual amount of ground. Another reason is that he does not oversimplify either himself or, despite his predilection for one-liners, his subject. Another reason is his humor, the various forms of which keep breaking through the surface in unexpected places, like wet-weather springs.

But the quality in him that I most prize, the one that removes him from the company of the writers I respect and puts him in the company, the smaller company, of the writers I love, is that he sees the gravity, the great danger, of the predicament we are now in, he tells it unswervingly, and he defends unflinchingly the heritage and the qualities that may preserve us. I read him, that is to say, for consolation, for the comfort of being told the truth. There is no longer any honest way to deny that a way of living that our leaders continue to praise is destroying all that our country is and all the best that it means. We are living even now among punishments and ruins. For those who know this, Edward Abbey's books will remain an indispensable solace. His essays, and his novels too, are "antidotes to despair." For those who think that a few more laws will enable us to go on safely as we are going, Abbey's books will remain—and good for him!—a pain in the neck.

William Eastlake

A Note on Ed Abbey

I first met Ed Abbey at my ranch in Cuba, New Mexico. I taught Ed how to ride and punch cattle. When the cattle started to punch back, Ed decided to become a writer. Ed discovered that to become a writer you must learn to drink a lot, which can be accomplished with much practice and dedication to the art. The art of drinking. What tempted Ed into the writing trade was what got the best of us into it. You can sleep late. Those who take writing seriously solemnly end up in Hollywood writing "The Guiding Light" and "Little House on the Prairie."

Ed decided early in life to save the planet, and he damn near did. First of all you have to learn to write well—which Ed did—then you have to bum around the country to discover who's going to blow us up—which Ed did. Then Ed set about blowing them up—and he did.

I went on one expedition with Ed outside of Flagstaff while Ed was working at Sunset Crater, and we carved down a huge Las Vegas girlie sign that was hiding the West. I can't say this is true, because that is illegal, but someone did it while we were in that area. Some bad people carved down all the expensive signs between Albuquerque and Santa Fe. I can't say we had anything to do with it, because such an act would be attacking the free-enterprise system. Ed would never attack the free-enterprise system that hides the West. He would never work against the game-of-grab system that rewarded him so generously. Ed called me to ask whether he should accept a tiny offer from a movie company to buy *The Brave Cowboy*. I told him it would probably have to be that small sum—or *nada*. Ed was broke when they paid a Hollywood scriptwriter a fortune and shot the film outside of Albuquerque and generously gave Ed a job as an extra. After that, Ed would never think of attacking the great American system that is dedicated to helping the struggling artist.

Ed was fortunate in his wandering to pick up some attractive characters such as Doug Peacock, who chose to live with a bunch of grizzly bears in Glacier Park and make his fight with them against the deadly white man. I recognize many of Ed's characters from real life whom he has, with his talent, made into alive-on-the-page people.

Ed, like the rest of us here in the boondocks, has not had much luck with the effete Eastern gang that controls the critics' pages. Ed frightens the critics. Ed does not fit into their charming literary world. Ed doesn't use big enough words. Worst of all, he wants to write about what's happening in America outside the suburbs of New York.

The New York publishers are cooperating with the Eastern gang and are careful not to overadvertise Ed's books, as though they don't want to be caught peddling such offensive writing that threatens the establishment, that threatens the conglomerate monopoly those publishers have become.

Why can't Mister Abbey write books that show the true beauty and the true manliness of the progressive spirit of the West? After all, Zane Grey and our own Louis L'Amour sell millions of copies of awesome literature that Duke Wayne would be proud to place on the silver screen. Can fifty million readers be wrong? Instead of writing about the picturesque characters that populate the colorful West, why does Mister Abbey continuously harp on the bulldozer burial of the West? Why does Mister Abbey attack the Park Service and the Forest Service that gave him the jobs that allowed him to write his books? You'd think Mister Abbey would appreciate a system that gave him the inside knowledge and the weapons to expose the big scam.

I visited Ed many times high in his swaying towers overlooking what's left of the National Forests. Ed scribbling away, trying to rescue the beauty that remains. We could see the plume from the distant smelter that formed black dollar signs as it wept its way toward the last of the West, sprinkling its acid rain as it went. Who cares? Just a few: Ed Abbey and his Monkey Wrench Gang. The kind of people who should be deported. Sent back where they came from.

Ed came from a small town in Pennsylvania called Home. Since I've known Ed he has been threatening to write about his hobo-like picaresque adventures in the rambling trade since leaving Home. I hope that's the book he tells me he is now on Page 900 of. If so, Thomas Wolfe was wrong. You can go home again. At least we can find out what happened to one of this country's best writers since he quit a place by that name. As Casey Stengel, that great Brooklyn Dodger philosopher, said in Stengelese, "I don't make predictions, especially about the future." Nevertheless, I hope the future weather charts predict less acid rain and more Edward Abbey.

Gregory McNamee

Scarlet "A"
on a Field of Black

I

Sunrise in Tucson, Arizona, red and purer than the dawn in Erewhon.

An incendiary light hugs the Santa Catalina Mountains, showers down on the survey stakes and luxury-condominium developments littering the pockmarked hillsides, and comes to rest on the reddish-gray bajada of the north slope, hard by the state prison farm. Cactus wrens, mockingbirds, and palomitas vie to make the loudest call over the thunder of sonic booms. Roadrunners peck at roadkills. A handful of desert bighorn, one of hundreds of endangered species inhabiting this place, scramble about the talus scatters. Below them electrified fences ringing intercontinental-missile silos glitter in the growing heat and intensity of light.

It is a typical Western town: slow, mean-spirited, xenophobic, pious, full of realtors, self-ordained ministers of crystal-worshipping pseudoreligions, bad artists, developers. Its transplanted economy is equally typical of the new American West: cattle, agribusiness, "clean" industry, some reclamation project or another, absentee landlordism. It is a place of failed dreams and tired acclimation to things as they are. A town full of the wrong kind of people in public office, the wrong kind of people in the welfare line, Tucson is a metaphor for something much larger.

This is Edward Abbey's home. It is an appropriate, if ironic setting: everything he hates and everything he loves converge and await together Abbey's first bleary uncoffeed gaze at the new morning. Murderousness, greed, and rapacity on the one hand; beauty, light, and the serenity of the desert on the other. And in between a truckstop or two and a banner, black, emblazoned with a monkey wrench.

Edward Abbey need not stray far from home to find an abundance of targets for his ready pen. What he requires to flesh out the subplot of a novel or the farther paragraphs of a political manifesto stands everywhere before him. Throw a rock from Abbey's study into the boomtown desert and, more often than not, you'll peg a cryptofascist, a snakeoil peddler, a land-rapist, a fundamentalist, a drifter out for a fast buck. The range of evils in boomtown Tucson is vast and seemingly endless—but not necessarily inescapable. Which is, I suppose, why Abbey likes it here.

II

All machines have their friction. But when the friction comes to have its machine, and oppression and robbery are organized, I say, let us not have such a machine any longer.

—HENRY DAVID THOREAU, 1849

Art cannot be separated from politics. The opinion that it can be, George Orwell reminds us, in itself constitutes a political position. Edward Abbey's writing cannot be fully understood without recognizing that a profound, little-known political conviction underlies and motivates it. To dispense with labels from the outset: in the realm of ideal politics, Edward Abbey is an anarchist.

The issue is not artificial. It arises because Abbey urges it to arise. For Abbey's books, from *Jonathan Troy* to *The Fool's Progress*, are communiques straight from the war zone— grown hopelessly close now—where the State opposes the individual, where the collectivist tendencies of modern nations, themselves becoming more and more alike, con- spire to crush those who wish to be left in peace.

The very term *anarchism* forces battle. Thanks to the mad French cafe bomber Ravachol and the inductive distortions of the propagandists who made of him a cause célèbre, the term conjures up a vision of deviance in the popular imag- ination. Endomorphic psychopaths mow down the inno- cent and the guilty alike with a crazed chuckle and a hot pipebomb; drunken proletarian mobs massacre priests on the altar and cart off the possessions of the hardworking middle class; blood flows in the gutter. Those whom anar- chism would displace keep such images current, essential to the popular definition of a political creed that means, at heart, "no rulers," not "no rule."

Abbey's anarchism departs from the vulgar characteriza- tions spawned by our media, our educators, our government. His anarchism is a positive force proclaiming the individual as the basis of civil society and trade. It is, he has written, nothing more than "democracy taken seriously." It holds that the one social necessity is absolute liberty for all. It rec- ognizes but one law: no person may aggress against another. It argues that governments are evil by their nature, commit- ting mass murder in the form of war, theft in the form of taxation. Because of the fundamentally antisocial character of the State, all governments, this anarchism maintains, must be abolished.

Edward Abbey's work, taken as a whole, can be seen as an unwavering meditation on that uncomplicated moral and political theory, one that proclaims its essence in Abbey's elegant formulation, "the root of all evil is the love of power." *The Monkey Wrench Gang*, his best-known novel, is an ode to individual liberty and the preservationist ethic of saving the land from a cancerous machine. *The Brave Cowboy* and *Good News* are thinly veiled exhortations to resist tyranny wherever it is met, by whatever means necessary. *Desert Solitaire* is a manifesto of the unchained soul, an inspired argument that human beings, like ecosystems, fare best when left alone. In Abbey's universe, art and politics are inseparable. In his words, "it is the writer's duty to hate injustice, to defy the powerful, and to speak for the voiceless." His writing is a call to arms.

III

If you understand your true mission and the very interests of art itself, come with us. Place your pen, your pencil, your chisel, your ideas at the service of the revolution.

—PETER KROPOTKIN, 1880

You cannot be free in a dying land if you lack the will to fight for its life—or to move on to fight elsewhere. You will not save the world or even a small corner of your soul through drunken, meaningless peroration to no one in particular. So Abbey posits in *Jonathan Troy*, his first novel, published in 1959, when he was thirty-two years old.

When the police have all manner of air cover and firepower and your spirit cannot brook jails or metropolises, strike out on your own for the wilderness, like the brave cowboy in Abbey's book of that name, where, if nothing else, you can establish "bases for guerrilla warfare against tyranny," as did the Monkey Wrench Gang.

When your rights are abrogated by the State and its hired guns there is but one thing to do: resist, even if resistance means your death. So Abbey, through John Vogelin, the hero of *Fire on the Mountain*.

Resist much, obey little.

Many other writers have said as much, among them Henry David Thoreau and Walt Whitman, but Abbey's pronouncements acquire a peculiar force today simply by virtue of their outlandishness. No one else is making them, at least through the vehicle of popular literature. The smart money among modern American writers is instead on tales of suburban passion, middle-aged angst, campus adultery, space rockets and demonically possessed Chryslers. It is not on telling readers, whom it is assumed should not be unduly challenged by ideas, that unless they shape up and begin to take responsibility for their own lives, they're going to wake up one morning to a ruined Earth and the crunch of truncheons—delivered with a California stylishness—slaves to a new order of machines and might. For all that's said and taught about the restorative and revolutionary power of words, few contemporary writers concern themselves with questions of social need and clear and present dangers to our liberty. For most, the audience is the narcoleptic and the voyeur, the future a shopping spree. Their duty, it seems, is less to their future than to their bankroll.

So if Edward Abbey writes with the distance of a prophetic voice crying in the wilderness, *vox clamatis in deserto*,

it is simply because he has so little immediate company.
Would that it were not so.

IV

Civilization is a youth with a Molotov cocktail in his
hand; culture is the Soviet tank or the L.A. cop that
guns him down.

—EDWARD ABBEY, 1968

Where the realm of ideal politics and that of the "real
world"—as self-styled pragmatists and apologists for things
as they are like to call it—coincide, one learns to expect
paradoxes. The range of human possibilities, after all, is cast
in relative terms; no party lines exist in nature (the claims
of sociobiology notwithstanding); black and white bound
a multitude of colors. Which is by way of prelude to saying
that Edward Abbey's books, despite their informed political vision, are not the place to go for a systematic, uncom-
promised philosophy of modern anarchism, where all ends
well and all contradictions melt into air, resolved by a handy
syllogism and a deft stroke of the pen. For that we have William Godwin, whose *Enquiry Concerning Political Justice* (1793)
prefigures John Vogelin's stand in *Fire on the Mountain*. We
have Pierre-Joseph Proudhon, whose *Qu'est-ce que la Propriété*
(1840) can be read as the first plank of the preservationism
Abbey has espoused in many speeches and essays. We have
Peter Kropotkin, whose marvelous *Memoirs of a Revolution-
ist* (1899) recounts a flight from the oppressive city echoed
years later by Will Gatlin of *Black Sun*.

Abbey is an artist, not a systematist; a novelist, not a
prophet. (Many of his readers, it seems, overlook these nice
distinctions.) Only once did he attempt to construct a

formal theoretical framework to justify his political positions, and that was long ago, and in another land: in 1959, when Abbey submitted to his graduate committee at the University of New Mexico a manuscript of some one hundred pages' extent to satisfy the requirement for the master's degree in philosophy. Entitled "Anarchism and the Morality of Violence," the unpublished manuscript comprises Abbey's exploration of the philosophical bases underlying anarchist theory and their relationship to the practicalities of making a revolution. Is the act of assassination, Abbey asks at the outset, morally justifiable? Abbey never tells us—after all, this is a school thesis, a form inhospitable to original thought in the place of received wisdom and surveys of the literature. Instead, he weighs the formulations of the great anarchist philosophers—Godwin, Proudhon, Bakunin, Kropotkin, and Sorel—to arrive at an academically defensible conclusion: assassination and other acts of political violence *may* be excused under a strict set of morally derived criteria, but they are never desirable. So much for Ravachol and Leon Czolgosz.

Abbey still holds to this view; it is mirrored in his fiction, as it is in his brief 1987 essay "Theory of Anarchy," written for the radical environmental journal *Earth First!*. The Monkey Wrench Gang, like the real-life ecoanarchists Abbey has inspired, is made up not of terrorists but saboteurs, latter-day Luddites who destroy machines instead of people, the exact counter to the practices of modern government. (Remember Jimmy Carter's neutron bomb.) In Abbey's work, no protagonist initiates acts of force, of violence against others. The only moral justification for violent acts—as in *The Monkey Wrench Gang* and *Good News*—is self-defense. It is not John Vogelin who brings warfare into the craggy mountains of western New Mexico, not George Hayduke

25

who fires from a multimillion-dollar helicopter gunship. That great symbol, the monkey wrench, is a tool made to be used on other tools, and not, like the billyclub, on people's heads. And it was not Edward Abbey who first came up with the notion of surgically bombing nonmilitary targets.

Violence is abhorrent, but it must remain an option in Abbey's world, fictional and real. That is the first paradox. How can the polarization necessary to a popular uprising against government be introduced without acts of force? How can one argue for civil war and at the same time maintain that political violence is ultimately unjustifiable?

There are no easy answers, surely none from Abbey himself. But there will be ample time and need to think of them, should Abbey's vision of the probable future be realized.

V

What reason have we Americans to think that our own society will necessarily escape the world-wide drift toward the totalitarian organization of men and institutions?

—EDWARD ABBEY, 1968

Recognize paradox, for it is your daily companion. There are no ready answers, no panaceas; perhaps there is not even hope. Make a stand and sooner or later you'll find yourself straddling a faultline—which is fine by Abbey.

Consider preservationism, for instance. Abbey often deals with this large issue, one that should be vital to modern anarchist theory. Preservationism—or "deep ecology," as it is sometimes known—calls for a fundamental revaluation of our attitudes toward the hierarchies of nature, of our place in the global ecosystem. It calls for humans to recognize themselves not as masters but as wards and caretakers of the planet. Preservationism demands the end of human government of wild lands and undomesticated species—the tamed world already being, it is feared, a total loss. In other words, preservationism is an ill-defined but universal anarchism taken beyond the purely social level. As the ecologist and writer Gary Paul Nabhan put it, "we must learn that we are but one of forty thousand vertebrate species and act accordingly."

Because a unified theory of preservationism has not been clearly set out, owing to the fearful tendency of leftists to tear apart organized approaches to anything, many questions go unanswered. In a stateless society, how are common lands and resources to be used? How are boundaries between the wild and the domesticated worlds to be determined? How are lands to be maintained and conserved? How shall humans obtain what they need? Who will decide? Within Abbey's preservationist ethic lies a tangle of dilemmas, and few hard answers—and, regrettably, few hard thoughts from other anarchists.

Under the slash-and-burn junta of Ronald Reagan, environmental theory has had increasingly to grapple with just such questions. As a result, it has polarized into two camps: those who would exploit all available resources, no matter where they might lie—public lands and legacies be damned—and those who, like Abbey, maintain that the only possible position to take on wilderness is to leave it alone, period. Throughout the Reagan years, thanks to James Watt, Donald Hodel, and other adherents to the clearcut and bulldoze school, the first position, however, gained the field, driven by mindless appeals to national security and blind patriotism: Do you want to see the nation sold down the river, after all, to the Saudis and the Japanese? Then let's rip apart the Rocky Mountains for shale oil right quick.

The Reaganite approach to wilderness has led the field only, it appears, because so few of Edward Abbey's fellow citizens are troubled by the prospect of a wilderness-free nation, so long as their resource needs—most of them not "needs" at all—are met, so long as their dependence can masquerade as the exercise of freedom of choice. There are still more recreational vehicles than environmentalists. Since anarchism, under which preservationism may one day be subsumed, is ideally the one truly democratic political ideology (no power for all), what can one do with the horrible impression that the polity would just as soon see a Disneyland built midway down the Grand Canyon as save Rainbow Bridge from further destruction or the continental shelf from offshore drilling? The paradox again.

Of course, Abbey's argument for wilderness preservation, outlined in *Desert Solitaire* and elsewhere, neatly sidesteps issues of aesthetics and the public good. His is romantic. We need wilderness, he says, not to inspire benevolence in our hearts but to stage wars of resistance when the going gets really bad, a point well understood by Fidel Castro, Mao, and Robert E. Lee. Whatever the case, Abbey has not proposed any real solution to the perfidious relationship between his countrymen and the land. He has instead gone in for skirmishing, as, for instance, when in recent years he has urged that cattle—hooved locusts, as he calls them—be removed from public lands throughout the American West, leading to a new range war, with ranchers everywhere howling for his blood.

Or consider immigration, on which Abbey's position has earned him even greater than his usual notoriety, at first in southern Arizona, and then nationwide. Abbey fired his opening shot in a letter to the *New York Review of Books* of December 17, 1981, in which, arguing from the "over-crowded lifeboat" theory, he called for an immediate halt to immigration into America, especially from Mexico and Central America. Abbey proposed that the current United States Border Patrol be expanded to a force of at least twenty thousand heavily armed guards, so that the American way of life might be made safe from the Mexican threat "to de-grade and cheapen [it] downward to the Hispanic standard."

Here the paradox arises ugly and mean. Anarchism, rec-ognizing no government, acknowledges no nation-state, and therefore no national borders. It further advances the right of freedom of movement and of self-determination. Anarchism—and, by extension, the practical anarchist—would cut its own throat were it to call in whatever way for increased State police power. Never mind the uncomfort-able overtones of racial superiority, for which anarchism can find no room, and which Abbey has yet to disavow.

In a series of letters to southern Arizona newspapers, Abbey later suggested that what he really wanted was for the Border Patrol to issue rifles and ammunition, gratis, to Mexican would-be immigrants at the border and to point them southward to Mexico City, where they might com-plete the aborted revolution begun seventy-five years ear-lier. The next several years saw Abbey further elaborating this argument, gleefully urging that the tide of immigrants from Latin America be turned away at the American fron-tier, while leftists, liberals, businesspeople, Mexican Amer-ican groups, conservatives, and Western congressmen joined battle against him in growing numbers. For all this, and per-haps because of the controversy he has inspired, Abbey remains a keen supporter of the closed border, writing letter after angry letter in support of the cause to anyone who might print them.

The paradoxical confluence of the real and the ideal. What else can one do but recognize it? After all, it has us hard by the throat, and it shows no sign of ever relaxing its grip.

But to recognize it is not to become its slave.

VI

Do I advocate another revolution? What do you mean, *another?* We have yet to see the first. But it's coming.

—EDWARD ABBEY, 1979

Tucson, Arizona. Edward Abbey's front yard.

Not Edward Abbey's American West, though, but Jimmy Carter's, Ronald Reagan's, Barry Goldwater's, James Watt's. Not the West of free rivers, unexplored mountain ranges, virgin forests, and open grasslands, but that of Glen Canyon Dam, the Central Utah Project, strip mines, clearcut hillsides, Los Angeles and a dozen more unsightly megalopolises. Not wilderness but human savagery. Not packmules but bulldozers. A West bristling with enemies—corporate capitalism, utilities, the Army Corps of Engineers, the Bureau of Land Management and the quisling Environmental Protection Agency, nuclear physicists, politicians, car dealers, developers—and without enough friends.

Things are pretty bad out here. There is no time left for writing to senators or for praying for the redemption of our souls. Things are bad. They're getting worse.

All this is a given. Because of the unabating rape of our land, because we are fast losing our American citizenship to that of violent new Sparta, if his past performance is a reliable guide, then Edward Abbey's politics and writing can become only angrier, more apocalyptic. The Western states, long accustomed to economic and political vassalage to Eastern capital, but also to a certain freedom hard to find elsewhere, are fast discovering that there is no longer room for the individual direction of a John Vogelin, the anarchic vision of an Edward Abbey.

That is why Abbey raises the black flag. That is why he writes: so that, in his words, "the fires of revolt may be kindled—which means hope for us all." Hope that some day we might live in a society of free men and women, tied responsibly and voluntarily to one another and to the Earth. Hope that we can put aside our violence and petty viciousness. Above all, hope that we can find it in ourselves to change the world.

James Hepworth

The Poetry Center
Interview

On February 2, 1977, Edward Abbey read for the University of Arizona Poetry Center's Visiting Writers Series in the Modern Languages Auditorium. Even before Abbey arrived, the seats in the auditorium were filled and latecomers sprawled in both aisles and crowded hallway entrances. Many of them carried copies of *The Monkey Wrench Gang*. When Lois Shelton, director of the Poetry Center, arrived with Abbey at her side, there was some talk of moving the reading elsewhere. Instead, Lois took the podium and asked people sitting in the aisles to move down toward the front of the auditorium. She introduced Abbey and invited the audience to meet the author over punch and cookies after the reading in the Terrace Room of the Student Union.

The applause that greeted Abbey came loud, long, and uproarious. I noticed a department head and an assistant dean standing on their chairs to see Abbey make his way to the stage. Within a few minutes both had left the building along with a small stream of their peers. Their seats were quickly taken, however, by those in the aisles nearest them.

What induced a department head and assistant dean to leave the reading produced a chorus of boos and shouts of encouragement from others in the audience, for Abbey opened the reading with a series of profane love songs he entitled "Love's Bawdy." "I'm not really a professional poet," he told his audience, "but I am living in your poet's cottage this week, so I am your official poet. God knows I've written a lot of poetry, but I've never published any of it anywhere. I think I'll read some of it to you so you'll understand why. . . . "

Mercifully, Abbey kept this part of the reading short. His method was to introduce each "poem" by dedicating it to a woman. Invariably, a woman in the audience by the same name would shriek or scream at the sound of "Ingrid" or "Bonnie" or "Clare" coming over the microphone. "No! Not *that* Clare," Abbey would insist, although he began each poem with an inquiry: "This one's for Ingrid. Is Ingrid here tonight?"

For most of the audience, Abbey's reading entertained and delighted. Others it outraged and incensed and even shocked. Notices in the local press afterwards were typically derogatory, as the opening sentences from even *Mountain Newsreal,* Tucson's most liberal monthly, indicate: "Edward Abbey should have stayed home last week to preserve his image as a cactus jumping Henry David Thoreau," wrote Margaret Hernandez. "Instead he came to Tucson to treat his audience to low-class erotic poetry, boring letters from his fans and his now-trite works condemning urban sprawl and smelter pollution."

As for myself, I was curious enough about Abbey after hearing him read to ask Lois Shelton to schedule an interview for me. Consequently, Lois arranged for Abbey and me to meet the next day over a tape recorder in Robert

Houston's undergraduate fiction class. I sent the transcribed interview to Abbey a few weeks later. Although he made a few small changes, what follows is nearly a literal transcription of our conversation.

In conversation Abbey is extraordinarily quiet and shy, a disarming contrast to the public Abbey and the image he has himself helped to create as a boisterous iconoclast. He speaks in low, even tones and listens carefully and attentively to questions. On this occasion he wore a deep blue V-neck sweater over a tan shirt, khaki pants, and low-heeled, round-toed boots.

ABBEY: I'm not responsible for anything I'm about to say.

HEPWORTH: When did you start writing? And how?

ABBEY: I suppose, like most activities, it began in childhood in various forms. I did my own comic books when I was a little kid. I went into journalism when I was in high school. I flunked the course, but I got interested in writing then. I was still interested in writing when I went to college. Sold my first piece about twenty-two years ago, so I feel that I've been at it all my life in one form or another.

HEPWORTH: You mentioned journalism last night. Do you consciously shift gears when you go from one genre to another?

ABBEY: I think I get more serious when I'm trying to write a piece of fiction. Perhaps that's why my fiction has not been so successful. When I'm writing an article or essay, I tend to think it's not very important, so I dash it off freestyle, more or less off the top of my head—or the bottom of my belly. I improvise, just dash along in any old manner that seems suitable to me. When I'm starting a piece of fiction, I do make a conscious decision about what sort of style I'm going to write it in, as well as what the story is going to be about. I'm not sure that's good, but I think that's been my practice so far.

HEPWORTH: You let the style more or less find itself. Do you think, then, that you have developed a journalistic style without making a conscious decision about it?

ABBEY: My journalistic style is pretty informal, I'd say; when I'm writing a piece of fiction, I tend to get a little more self-conscious, and try to make the style fit the subject matter and vice versa. I think you can see that in the novels that I've written, if you've read them. It seems to me that each one is written in a different style.

HOUSTON: Do you make a distinction between style, tone, and voice?

ABBEY: No, by the word *style*, I mean to include those terms.

HEPWORTH: Who are your favorite contemporary American journalists?

ABBEY: In the field of journalism, I'm a Hunter S. Thompson freak. I do admire his work. I would have to admit I like Tom Wolfe's stuff, too, but I don't like his point of view. And in fiction, I like Tom McGuane. Have you read *Ninety-Two in the Shade? The Bushwhacked Piano?* He also wrote the screenplay *Missouri Breaks*, which is kind of well-known. A lousy film—I thought—but I like the three novels he's done so far. I'm an admirer of William Eastlake, who used to teach here. He's also an old friend of mine, but I do think he's a good writer. I think I've learned a lot from him. I see traces of his influence in my stuff. Who else? Pynchon. I like *Gravity's Rainbow*. I didn't understand it, of course, but I was fascinated by it.

In fact, one night I was sitting in my little hut out in Arivaipa Canyon when I was a caretaker out there. I was trying to finish *Gravity's Rainbow*. I was on page 780 or so, forty or fifty more pages to go. I was sitting on the couch in my little trailer house out there, and a scorpion crawled out from underneath the couch and stung me on the foot, and I got up and—Oh, I hate to admit it—but I stepped on that poor old scorpion. Got mad. And so I killed the scorpion. Then I went in the kitchen and filled the basin with ice cubes and water and went back to the couch and put my stung foot in that basin of icewater and went on and finished the book. I just couldn't stop. Probably by that time I was weighted on compulsion just to get through the damn thing. After you've read 700 pages . . .

HEPWORTH: What about Stegner?

ABBEY: Well, I did read Stegner's biography of Powell, but I don't think I've read any of his fiction. Have you people read a collection called *The Neon Wilderness* by Nelson Algren? They're fine little stories.

HEPWORTH: How about Frank Waters?

ABBEY: Oh, I don't like Waters's style very much. I read *The Man Who Killed The Deer* a long, long time ago, in my student days back in the '50s. It didn't attract me. Something about Waters' style. It's too . . . what? Fancy? Overblown?

HEPWORTH: Romantic?

ABBEY: Yeah. I read the book he wrote about the Colorado River and disliked it for similar reasons. He maintains a constant high pitch and intensity and fine, fancy rhetoric, it seems to me. I prefer writers who can range over a whole scale of tones and voices, who can go from the burlesque to the bawdy to the sublime, poetical. I think Pynchon has that ability. I think that's one reason his books interest me so much.

HEPWORTH: What do you think of Gore Vidal's work?

ABBEY: I like his essays very much. I think he is a brilliant essayist, critic, reviewer. Certainly, I admire his wit, his sharp tongue. I've read a few of his novels and didn't like them very much. He's certainly a competent writer, no question about that. His things are perfectly written, but they seem to lack some sort of basic passion. They're amusing, witty, well done, but he's just not the kind of writer that I very much admire. I like Steinbeck, Céline. I like writers who are sort of half-crazy at best. I think it does help to be crazy, and I think Vidal is much too sane and rational a person to be a great novelist.

HEPWORTH: Do you think the things you've written, particularly your conservation articles published in magazines with enormous readerships like *Playboy* and *Audubon*, have altered the way people think, say, about strip mining?

ABBEY: I doubt it. I don't think written propaganda makes much difference in a war. I got a lot of letters from that article in *Playboy* you're referring to, both pro and con. I was very flattered to get hate letters from Senator Hanson of Wyoming and from Senator Moss of Utah, from the president of the American Coal Association and an official of the EPA . . . all those fellows wrote in condemning the article, which was quite delightful to me, of course.

HEPWORTH: How about *Monkey Wrench Gang*? Have you had much response from that?

ABBEY: No, no official reaction at all.

HEPWORTH: Are the characters in that book inspired by real people?

ABBEY: Yes, to some extent. You might say they are inspired by people I know. They're not portraits of anybody I know. I borrowed a lot of things for each of those people: attitudes, style of language, occupations, even physical appearance. But I would still insist that they are not portraits. I just borrowed what was useful to create the fictional characters.

HEPWORTH: Is there a movie in the process for that book?

ABBEY: There's an option on the book. Whether they'll actually raise the money to make a film out of it, I don't know. Hollywood options far more books than they ever get around to filming.

HOUSTON: How do you feel they did by you with *Lonely Are The Brave?*

ABBEY: I like that film. I think that they did pretty well. Dalton Trumbo wrote the screenplay. He followed the book. He didn't change the story very much. They deleted a lot of the long-winded, philosophizing dialogue, jail cell scenes. I think they made a good movie.

HEPWORTH: Did you consider taking a part in it?

ABBEY: I did have a part in it. I was one of the sheriff's deputies. I still get a check every year from the Screen Actor's Guild for about $4.55. As long as they keep running it on TV I guess I'll receive one.

HEPWORTH: Did they ask you to script the movie?

ABBEY: No, I was hurt by that. They bought that book several years after it was published. They only paid me $7,500 for it. I think they felt a little guilty about that. When they began filming it, they hired me as a consultant. I persuaded them to use the Albuquerque, New Mexico, setting for the actual filming, same as in the story, so they hired me to show them around the town, show them where the roads and trails were in the mountains, out on West Mesa. It was the best job I ever had in my life. They paid me $100 a day and all expenses. Of course, the job only lasted three days. And they also gave me this bit part and a sheriff's deputy's costume, a leather jacket and a gun full of blanks. No speaking part.

HOUSTON: Do you market your own stuff?

ABBEY: No, I've got an agent in New York. . . . He's the only agent I've ever had. I've had a few publishers complain to me about what a ruthless man he is, so I guess he's good.

HOUSTON: When you do non-fiction, do you go looking for ideas? Do you say, "Hey, I need six or seven hundred bucks. It's time to do an article!" Or do you just write when you feel like writing?

ABBEY: Well, ever since I published *Desert Solitaire*, I've been writing magazine articles on commission. The editors approach me. That's how I sort of got stuck in this rut—because of that one book. I never wanted to be an environmental crusader, an environmental journalist. I wanted to be a fiction writer, a novelist. Then I dashed off that *Desert Solitaire* thing because it was easy to do. All I did was copy out of some journals that I'd kept. It was the first book that I published that had any popularity at all, and at once I was put into the "Western Environmentalist Writer" bag, category, pigeonhole. I haven't tried very hard to get out of it. I've been making a pretty easy living at it since then.

HOUSTON: You don't really mind taking the commissions as they come up? You don't ever say, "No. That doesn't interest me"?

ABBEY: I've turned down a few. Not very many. Time-Life wanted me to write a book about the Okeechobee Swamp. I decided to hell with that.

HEPWORTH: Is publishing fiction a problem for you? As you said yourself a moment ago, your work has been pigeonholed. We tend to think of you as an environmentalist writer. Don't publishers tend to demand more of the same, more of what will sell?

ABBEY: I haven't had that problem yet. I've been able to publish most of the fiction I've written. Most of the fiction, too, has had a western or southwestern setting. It's been, at least to some extent, concerned with environmental issues, I guess you could say. I haven't been able to avoid that. The novel I'm trying to finish is a futuristic western set in Phoenix about the year 1999, after The Great Collapse. Horses are grazing on Van Buren, Gila monsters scampering up and down Central Avenue.

HEPWORTH: Is that a wistful vision or a frightening vision?

ABBEY: The way my story is going, there's a massive struggle going on over the control of Phoenix, over whether or not Phoenix should be rebuilt. Some are trying to help Phoenix rise from its ashes. The other faction is trying to finish burning it down. It's about a regional civil war.

HOUSTON: Are you taking sides?

ABBEY: Implicitly. I suppose you could call it a novel of political ideas, essentially. Anarchy versus Order.

HOUSTON: But you're not going to tell us which side you're on?

ABBEY: Well, I'm trying to be fair, trying not to stack the deck—too much.

HEPWORTH: Are you satisfied with your writing?

ABBEY: I keep hoping I can do better. I have the feeling that I've never put my best effort into a book. Maybe that's illusion. It seems to me everything I've written has been too easy, did not require much effort.

HEPWORTH: Last night during your reading you said something to the effect that every novelist fancies himself a poet. Do you read poetry? Do you write poetry seriously?

ABBEY: Oh, yes! I've written a lot of very serious, very intense poetry, and I was tempted to try that out on you last night. Chickened out. I don't think any of it was good enough to try to publish, but I would like to write poetry. I think maybe I could.

HEPWORTH: Do you think the reading public and publishers themselves are more receptive than they used to be to fiction written about the West?

ABBEY: I don't know. I think it is still a handicap to write about the West. It's hard to get critics and reviewers to take any book with a western setting seriously. They're always tempted to dismiss it as some kind of *western* literature, much as women's books are dismissed: "Oh, here's another Women's Book. . . . " Once you give a book a western setting and you fail to populate it with stereotypes, publishers might not be so interested. If you're going to write a serious book about big city life, well, they would say, then you had better get back to New York. We may be able to overcome that, eventually.

HEPWORTH: How?

ABBEY: Well, I think Eastlake has had some success at it. I think his novels are taken quite seriously by the eastern critics. Of course, he was also smart enough to write a couple of war novels to show that he could do that, too.

HOUSTON: Eastlake always comes down on the "right" side, too. His characters aren't bad, but his Indians are what publishers want to hear about Indians. . . .

ABBEY: Yeah, his Indians are fantasy creatures. . . .

HEPWORTH: Probably no other two groups have been any more affected by prevaricated models of themselves than the American Indian and the Anglo born or raised in the West.

42

ABBEY: Yeah. Some Vietnam war veterans have told me that the most popular TV show in Vietnam was *Combat*. They said many of the soldiers used to sit around the set and watch the series to see how it was done, see how they were supposed to talk. Go to any small town drugstore. You'll see all the paperbacks are westerns.

HEPWORTH: Yes. Even the people who should know better still refuse to see the West as anything other than the Last Frontier.

ABBEY: I guess the westering myth is the nearest thing to a national myth we can ever create in the country. It's very possible. It may never be possible to overcome it, or get away from it. Maybe it's not even desirable. Maybe literary historians five hundred years from now will decide that Zane Grey and Louis L'Amour were the most important American writers.

HEPWORTH: Did I hear you say that you once taught writing?

ABBEY: I presided over a writing sweatshop up in Salt Lake City one time. I only tried it that once. Maybe I could do it better with a little experience. I didn't quite feel I was giving the kids their money's worth. I could read their stuff and say, "This is all right, or this is terrible, or . . ." I don't have any analytical or critical talent for pointing to exactly what's wrong with somebody's work, for telling them how to improve it. I also found it hard to get interested. I got discouraged. One poor guy, I'm sure, I discouraged from writing forever. He wrote a Mormon love story. I read it aloud to the class. (It was my policy to read everybody's work myself, and in that way it could get a fair and impartial reading.) I read this guy's Mormon love story, and I couldn't help laughing at all the wrong places. For half the story the hero agonized over whether or not to kiss the girl.

43

HEPWORTH: Some writers wake up and they find out that the public knows who they are, that they have a kind of image or myth they're supposed to live up to. All of a sudden, some writers who find this out start playing games. Does your recognition ever tempt you or ever bother you?

ABBEY: Oh, I'm dimly aware of some sort of mythical Edward Abbey, but I don't take him seriously, don't attempt to live up to it. I'm surprised that anyone would ever want to meet me because I don't live up to the characters in my books, don't try to. It sometimes seems to me that the Edward Abbey who writes these articles and books and so on is just another fictional creation, not much resemblance to the real one, to the one I think I know. The real Edward Abbey—whoever the hell that is—is a real shy, timid fellow, but the character I create in my journalism is perhaps a person I would like to be: bold, brash, daring. I created this character, and I gave him my name. I guess some people mistake the creation for the author, but that's their problem.

597ax

This is a dreadful room. Of course, every classroom I've seen here is dreadful—the same greyish-white walls, the same tan cork bulletin boards covered with advertisements for research-paper services and *Time* and evenings of introduction to Transcendental Meditation. In the worst of them the desks are bolted to the floor and the students sit trapped in rows staring at the backs of one another's heads. In the best, the seminar rooms, students sitting around grey formica tables in turquoise vinyl chairs may at least look one another in the face. This room is halfway between—the desks grip one in the middle tight as jaws, but at least they're movable. In theory, we could push them into a circle and face each other; in practice, we leave them in ragged rows and stare ahead at the teacher.

He stands at the front of the room gravely. In my journal I jot, "Rugged. Handsome. Grey-bearded." Just my image of a park ranger. He writes long lists on the chalkboard, which we copy into notebooks.

He recommends magazines: *The New Yorker, The New York Review of Books, Atlantic, Harper's, Esquire, Nation, New*

Republic, National Review, Mother Jones, Rocky Mountain Magazine, Outside.

He recommends essayists: Montaigne, Orwell, White, Thoreau.

He asks us to buy, read, and review three of the following: Edward Hoagland, *Reader*; Joan Didion, *Slouching Toward Bethlehem, The White Album*; Nora Ephron, *Scribble, Scribble*; Joseph Wood Krutch, *Best Nature Writing, Krutch Omnibus*; John McPhee, *Reader*; Alan Harrington, *The Immortalist, Psychopaths*; Wendell Berry, *The Long-Legged House, The Unsettling of America*; Barry Lopez, *Of Wolves and Men, Desert Notes, River Notes*; Michael Herr, *Dispatches*; Hunter Thompson, *Fear and Loathing in Las Vegas, The Great Shark Hunt*; Tom Wolfe, *The Right Stuff, Mauve Gloves . . .* ; James Baldwin, *Notes of a Native Son*; Edward Abbey, *Abbey's Road, The Journey Home*; Lewis Thomas, *The Lives of a Cell, The Medusa and the Snail*; Annie Dillard, *Pilgrim at Tinker Creek*; Norman Mailer, *Presidential Papers, Cannibals and Christians*; William Zinsser, *On Writing Well.*

When he has finished the lists, he asks by way of dismissal, "Are there any questions?"

Everyone looks blank. Notebook paper shuffles. Then someone says, "Yes. What should we call you?"

"Mr. Abbey," he says. "You should call me Mr. Abbey."

In return he calls us Ms. Mairs, Mr. Kessler, Mr. Moneyhun, Mr. Hepworth, Ms. Miller, Mr. Barwell. . . . Perhaps he has been told, as I was my first year of teaching, that one must run a class on a last-name basis in order to maintain respect. Or perhaps he is imitating, as most teachers do, the pedagogical style of his own professors.

I don't like to be called Ms. Mairs. A few people call me Mrs. Mairs—those students who still believe that some pigs are more equal than others, and the women on the telephone who try to sell me carpet-cleaning for my carpetless house. But I don't like titles, which reinforce distinctions and distances among people, thereby creating space for patterns of domination; and I refer to myself only as Nancy. I don't know if any of my classmates share my political objections, but they must be a little baffled at the formality—manners are pretty casual at this university, as I guess they're bound to be anywhere that the climate permits students to come to class more than half-naked most of the year. Once I've seen a student's navel, I find it hard to call him "Mr. Holmes."

The matter of names presents a tonal problem, but the class has structural difficulties as well. For one thing, we have no texts. In other workshops, we hand out copies of our work the week before discussing them, but here we read them aloud. I write in my journal, "Abbey's workshop. I like being entertained by people reading to me aloud, but I can't possibly retain enough of what I hear to offer any criticism." The penalty for literacy—for turning composition into a written rather than an oral art—is that we no longer learn to listen as acutely as we read. In consequence, discussion here tends to be vague, desultory.

The problem is exacerbated by the motley make-up of the group. Most of the members are in the M.F.A. program, but some write poetry and some fiction. A couple of us, having taken the M.F.A., are working toward the Ph.D. A couple more are undergraduates, wide-eyed young women who drop out before the end of the semester—daunted, perhaps, by the amount of work required. Three to six typewritten pages due every Monday, including the three book reviews, a magazine review, and an interview. Edward Abbey doesn't fool around.

Such a mixture could be enlivening, but it isn't. At this university—maybe at every such institution—division is the underlying principle. Artists from scientists, "creative writers" from "critics," poets from fiction-writers from essayists. If you try to straddle, you're likely to end up drawn and quartered. This class operates on just such a principle. One of the members will later say to me in a letter, "The answer [to his difficulty in finding a teaching job] lies in separating writing instruction from English Departments altogether. I'd like to quarantine the lit. people in separate Literature Depts. Perhaps these can be integrated into departments of Archeology or even Museum Science, if there is such a thing." Everyone here is a little suspicious of what everyone else is doing.

I know all these things because I've been a graduate student here enough years that my longevity is an embarrassment. Edward Abbey has just come.

Whether because of the strain of formality or the lack of texts or the motley membership, the class isn't working. One day we move to The Big A, a beer-and-hamburger joint near campus, where we sit around a long wooden table facing each other; but one of us tells the English Department, and it turns out that meeting off-campus violates university regulations. So we squeeze back into our desks, drooping and drowsing in our stuffy fluorescent room.

Complaints about the class have begun almost immediately, the kind of generalized bitching that makes me furious. Especially when it's done by graduate students, who bear a heavy responsibility, it seems to me, when a class goes badly. I am more patient with teacher-dependence in my freshmen. But we're not bewildered freshmen. Several of us, in fact, are experienced and capable teachers. It's up to us, I tell some of the gripers, to make the class work.

I don't exactly put my money where my mouth is. I've been messing up my life, and I've withdrawn now to the remotest corner of myself, where I spend a lot of time gazing out of the window at a couple of trees against the dark-rose bricks of the College of Education and jotting acerbic notes in my journal. "Earth-maiden . . . has brought her dog, who whistles in his sleep or wanders around, nails clicking on the linoleum." "Alan Harrington, author of *The Immortalist*, is here. We are talking about the possibility of living forever. Not something of lively interest to a suicide." "Clyde has read a piece on Indians. Some discussion of 'Indians,' limited to a few people. Jim says, 'It's too late to leave the Apaches alone.' Let's. Let's leave the Apaches alone." Later I will feel sorry for my tightness, my distance, my lack of generosity.

Slowly the class begins to improve. We seem not so wary of each other, and we are working out ways of discussing pieces we only hear. Ed relaxes, his shyness now natural and close-fitting, not a piece of armor. One day he reads us his own work, an essay on Arivaipa Canyon which will appear later in *Down the River*, and we are reassured of his involvement in the struggle. It's late, but we've begun the process of supporting one another in our work. I begin to think that textlessness has advantages. The focus in most workshops is too often narrow, nitpicking, negative, a piece scrutinized for its shortcomings rather than its successes. Here our vision is necessarily diffuse, our responses impressionistic and global. We act as appreciators of one another's ventures, a true audience.

Uncertain at the outset in the classroom, Ed is from the first a sure-handed editor, thorough, tough, and good-humored. This last quality I tax to the extreme. New to prose-writing, except for academic purposes, and engaged in the study of women's autobiography, I use this class to buy time for experimentation. I start generating a dreary, static reminiscence of a house in my childhood, which I dole out in dribs and drabs, whatever I've written in a week. After the first drib, Ed writes, "Keep going with it." After the second, he's getting itchy: "Dear Ms. Mairs, this stuff is getting too vague, a bit boring. . . . What's your point? . . . You need some laughs in this here opus. And—contrary to Nabokov—some *ideas*. Of course you can't please everybody, but in *this* course you have only to please me." At the end of twenty pages, he's done in: "I can understand that your reminiscences seem precious to you, as mine do to me, but somehow you've got to find a way, a device, a meaning, to make these memoirs readable to an ordinary bored, busy, hard-nosed, cynical, weary, cigar-smoking, whisky-drinking, fornicating old fart like—not me!—but your typical magazine or book editor. In its present form it will not sell. Maybe you don't care about that, and that's okay, but still, your primary obligation as a writer is to give pleasure, to entertain, or at least to instruct. Now if you were (already) a famous person this might not matter; but you're not; so it does." I'm exhausted too.

But I don't reform. I do a couple of short pieces—and they work—and then suddenly, grief-stricken at the death of a kitten, I'm spewing a lifetime of memories of cats. Ed likes cats, and he bears up well. But finally he has to plead for mercy: "OK, very charming, but this cat saga is getting too long & complicated. Why not dash off the assigned book reviews, and the interview, as requested, and we'll call it quits for 597ax 1981." If I were he, I don't think I could be so polite in the face of certain death by smothering in particolored fur.

It's almost the end of the semester, and Ed is looking decidedly haggard. He's been teaching three workshops a week—the other two for undergraduates—and no doubt editing all the submissions with the same painstaking attention he's given to mine. Nine hours a week in the classroom, probably three times that wielding a red pencil. When, I wonder, does he do any work of his own?

Probably never, if my experience is any gauge. Writing and teaching are two of the most incompatible activities I know, because they eat up the same sort of creative energy, require the same imaginative structuring of experience for an audience. What you give to your students—and if you're any good, you give a hell of a lot—you don't have left for the blank page. And teaching is seductive, because the audience is live. They respond. They draw more and more out of you, tap more and more of your reserves, the time and effort you meant to spend elsewhere, elsewhen. If you let them. I let them, and I know a lot of other writers who do too.

Perhaps any work other than writing is bad for the writer: Melville suffered, no doubt, on account of the bills of lading; and T.S. Eliot had to be bought out of the bank by his friends. But, having done other things, I think teaching especially dangerous. And nowadays, with writing programs and workshops and conferences flourishing, an increasing number of writers are getting sucked into it. Some resolve the dilemma by teaching badly: reading students' manuscripts sloppily or not at all, dashing off hasty and superficial comments, holding classes erratically. Most, too conscientious for such an easy resolution, live like jugglers, trying to keep the poem, the novel, the essay from smashing into the ground.

Desert Solitaire wasn't jotted down on Monday afternoons after two and a half hours of 597ax. Nor was *The Monkey Wrench Gang*. If some of *Down the River* gets written during this semester, it does so despite, not because of, Clyde's Indians and my cats. The better teacher Ed becomes, the more tempted I am to burst into his office, shouting and shooing: "Off with you! Now! Go breach a dam. Lock the door behind you. And lose the key."

End of the semester. We're all looking a little haggard now, as everyone does at the end of fifteen weeks of teaching/ writing. The last day of class, English Department policy be damned, we gather at Ed and Clarke's house on the desert's edge and drink beer. Away from the fluorescent lights, the pink and green plastic desks, with the promise of a long break only a week away, we seem buoyant in spite of the sudden heat that leaves you gasping in surprise, spring after spring, in this immoderate climate.

A handful of us are left at dinner time, so we grill some hot dogs over a fire on the patio and wrap them in tortillas and wash them down with more beer. The sun has pitched over the edge of the Tucsons, leaving their saw-toothed profile flat and purplish against the greening sky. Venus pricks through, not far from a sliver of moon. I suppose we talk, but later when I picture the scene it will be a silent still, a few blurred blue silhouettes against the coming stars.

Finally we scatter. In the calm air outside the city sounds seem thin and sharp, car doors slamming, voices calling. "Goodnight." "Goodnight." "Great party." "See you soon." "Goodnight." "Thanks, Ed."

David Remley

Fire on the Mountain

"The story which follows," writes Edward Abbey in a prefatory note to *Fire on the Mountain*, "was inspired by an event that actually took place in our country, not many years ago." Abbey was very likely thinking about the predicament of old-time New Mexico rancher John Prather, who stood off the whole United States Government when it tried to add his ranch to a rocket testing range. Prather's battle was like that of New Mexico rancher Dave McDonald, who recently returned illegally to his home on the missile range and announced that he intended to possess his ranch or be fully compensated for the loss of it. This battle between the government and southern New Mexico ranchers has been going on for many years, ever since World War II, when the military base developed at Alamogordo. In order to acquire land for firing ranges, the United States filed condemnation suits against ranchers. Although most of the ranchers considered fighting eviction, most gave in and moved off the land which they and, in some cases, their families had possessed for two or three generations. John Prather, unlike the others, decided never to give in, but to fight removal with a Winchester if it came to that.

Prather's story, told in detail in C.L. Sonnichsen's book *Tularosa: Last of the Frontier West*, is really the story of the confrontation between a government which represents an abstraction known as "the national interest" and those individual Americans who have devoted years of dreaming, risking, and working to make a livelihood and a home on the land. As someone stated the irony of the situation: Prather was "the kind of man who built the nation the missile men were expecting some day to defend." The Prathers themselves had come to New Mexico from Texas in 1883. Soon after the turn of the century, John and his brother Owen moved out onto open range land south of the Sacramento Mountains and began building up their own ranches. Owen was a sheepman, but John was a cattleman, the true old Texas type. Over nearly fifty years, relying on his own stubbornness and his own sweat—the tradition among ranchers—John Prather built up a spread he was proud of: four thousand acres deeded plus twenty thousand leased for grazing from the state and the federal governments. His home place included a good rock house, cattle trails, fences, a one thousand and fifty foot well, corrals, loading chutes, and stock tanks which John had scraped out of the land with a team and scoop. After he had built all this and thus made it his, the United States Government came along and ordered him off. It needed his place to test rockets so that they could some day protect him and other Americans. John Prather, however, was accustomed to protecting himself. He had never asked others to do that for him, and this was *his* place. He did not intend to move. "I'm not moving," he said simply, following legal proceedings against him at Albuquerque in the summer of 1956.

John Prather was the epitome of the old-time western cattleman. His code of conduct was the very essence of self-reliance, determination, and endless hard work on the land. To his mind, these qualities put into practice made a ranch his. When the government sent out a marshal to evict him, he stood off the marshal and his deputies with a knife until they gave it up and went away. On another occasion he barricaded himself in his rock house and said, "I will kill the first man that steps into the door of my house. I'm staying here, dead or alive." Finally, the government, undoubtedly having decided he wasn't worth the fight and knowing that eventually it'd get his land anyway, let him have the victory. He stayed on the home place. He did not want the money offered him for it. "If they come after me, they better bring a box," he said. In February, 1965, John Prather died in an Albuquerque hospital where he had been forced to go for medical care. Afterward, the government absorbed his ranch.

Fire on the Mountain forces us to examine all the issues of ownership, possession of the land, and the rights of private citizens which individuals like John Prather and Dave McDonald embody, an examination which is an outgrowth of what Gerald Haslam calls Abbey's "concern with human freedom in an industrial society." The issues Abbey dramatizes may be divided into two separate but closely related sets. One of these develops from Abbey's belief that ownership and making a home mean living on the land and working it, in short, being committed to it, so that finally and somewhat ironically the owner is himself possessed. The Box V and Thieves Mountain possess Grandfather Vogelin much as the same country had possessed the Apache before him. Vogelin must therefore defend the land, just as the Apache had, with violence if necessary. "If I have to give in I'm going to give in like an Apache. That's part of the pattern," he tells Lee Mackie. "That's the tradition around here." If Vogelin's ancestor stole Thieves Mountain from the Apache, he used their methods to do it. These were direct and violent and honest in a very primary sense of that word. Vogelin cannot therefore communicate very well with a government agent, a legal salesman like Colonel DeSalius, who comes out all smiles and cordiality in a well pressed wash'n'dry suit to present legal papers for the taking of the Box V.

Clearly, in Abbey's view, legal paperwork cannot constitute true ownership any more than modern men, representing urban-industrial development and promoting abstractions like "the national interest," can be possessed by land, or be worthy of the true commitment which making a home and being independent require. DeSalius, for all his education, his confidence and experience, for all his slick legal arguments, is totally unaware of what he is really trying to take from the old man. He does not even like Vogelin's country. "Good God, this is a horrible place," he exclaims in his one show of emotion in the entire story, as, his argument rejected for the last time, he walks away from his final meeting with Vogelin. DeSalius and the government he represents are legal thieves; but they would steal by paperwork rather than by personal risk. They are not within the tradition of the Apache and Thieves Mountain.

The other set of issues Abbey dramatizes is perhaps only barely implied in the personal battle of John Prather to keep his ranch. This cluster of issues, like that of individual rights in an industrial society, is one of Abbey's central concerns. It is generated by his interest in wilderness and what the twentieth century's uses of it ultimately mean for natural life and human life on this planet. *Fire on the Mountain* is a hymn of praise to the spirit of the wild manifest in Thieves

Mountain and the lion—the last lion left on Grandfather's place—and to the spirit of Grandfather Vogelin, who is himself a lion of a man. The novelette attempts to stretch our awareness of the wild, godlike beauty and spirit which is in the land and which Vogelin shares.

Abbey's choice of the figure of the old-time cattleman to dramatize his central issues of individual rights and of awareness of wilderness is a fortunate one artistically. The figure of the frontier cattleman has a special symbolic power which other historical western figures lack—the miner, the railroader, the sodbuster, or the engineer. The cattleman depended upon the grass for his livelihood. The other figures are known for developing the land, for turning it into something other than what it was. The cowman needed his land fresh and well-watered as possible, unspoiled, untampered with. He used roads and trails, and he often favored the coming of railroads, but he didn't ordinarily want them cutting into his rangeland. He was quite happy to drive his cattle to a central shipping point. He fenced, but only in order to protect his grass. The true cattleman knew that overgrazing was a terrible hazard; it destroyed the grass, eroded the land. While he was not in the business for esthetic purposes, he nonetheless understood the needs of the land and spent his days looking after them. Grandfather Vogelin, like Homer Bannon in Larry McMurtry's *Horseman, Pass By*, is an aged version of a true cattleman. Having lived on the Box V for a lifetime, he has both made it his and been possessed by it, by the land, the mountain, and the lion. "Whose mountain? Whose land? Who owns the land?" Lee asks. "I am the land," the old man answers. "I've been eating this dust for seventy years. Who owns who? They'll have to plow me under."

The cattleman's means of covering the land and of working his cattle—on horseback—also has a special artistic significance for Abbey's novelette. As Larry McMurtry, John Graves, Stan Steiner and others have pointed out in writing about the cattleman and the cowboy, the figure of a man on horseback has captured the imagination since ancient times. That figure suggests a freedom, a boldness and dignity associated with heroic times, and especially an intimacy with nature which a figure traveling afoot nearly always lacks. Grandfather Vogelin as horseman (he and Billy and Lee are hardly ever afoot in *Fire on the Mountain*) is therefore an almost perfect choice to represent the magnificent land he moves so freely about. Billy, too, improves as horseman under the guidance of Lee and of Grandfather. Early in the story Billy is "scared" of the horses being readied for the day's work. But he bridles and saddles Old Blue without help from the men and, after getting knocked down by the hungry horse, mounts up, touches the horse's sides, moves forward, and feels "about ten feet tall, a master of horses and men."

Fire on the Mountain, like *The Brave Cowboy*, reveals imaginative uses of the myth of the cowboy, a myth which, in its most familiar forms, has been heavily overused in pop western formula novels, in the movies and on TV serials. In *Fire on the Mountain* Abbey uses the walk-down shootout popularized by Owen Wister in *The Virginian* and immortalized in countless reenactments of shootouts at the OK Corral. In the pop version, the bad cowboy insults the good one. Trampas makes dark remarks about the Virginian. Given until sundown to leave town, the Virginian cannot ignore the insult. His reputation would suffer. He would be thought a coward. Since "there was no way out, save only the ancient, eternal way between man and man" and since to resort to legalities in such "personal matters" would be "the great mediocrity," the shootout must come. In Abbey's novel, however, both the issues and the characters involved are very different than in the stock version. The marshal has arrived at the Box V to storm the place. Vogelin has barricaded the headquarters and refuses to give up. The marshal and his deputies, representing "the national interest," teargas the house to drive the old man out. Sporadic shooting occurs. Lee Mackie arrives from town, leaps from his big car, throws orders at the officers, and strides up onto the front porch of the house. When Lee calls to the old man to come out, Vogelin appears in the door, Winchester aimed at Lee's belly. The two face one another, Lee weaponless. "I'll kill you," Vogelin shouts. "Here I am," Lee says. He spreads his arms toward Grandfather. But Vogelin cannot pull the trigger on his old friend. Defeated, he throws down his rifle, calls Lee a "dirty traitor," and slumps forward into his arms.

Abbey's shootout is no simple two-way situation with easily identified issues. The marshal and his deputies are employees paid to represent an abstraction, "the national defense effort," DeSalius calls it. They are not traditional bad guys, but mercenaries. There have been no personal insults; no reputation has been threatened. Lee has absolutely nothing to gain from the frightening risk he takes (being a lifelong hunter he, of all people, would have known the unforgettable mess a Winchester makes at close range). Throughout the story, Abbey characterizes Lee Mackie as one raised in the shadow of Thieves Mountain, a man who has "seen the lion," who clearly loves and respects Vogelin (he hauls his horse out from town regularly to ride with the old man), but who is also trying to live in the modern world. Not originally of that world, he has chosen to try to settle with it so as to have some control over his situation in it.

Fire on the Mountain asks who is worthy of owning the land and what possession means. But it is primarily a story about *seeing* the land, a book to stretch one's awareness of what is out there. From early in the story it is clear that Billy has already been invited into the company of men who see. "Brightest New Mexico," he says. "In that vivid light each rock and tree and cloud and mountain existed with a kind of force and clarity that seemed not natural but supernatural." Minutes later, driving with Grandfather toward the Box V, Billy says: "Each summer for three years I had come to New Mexico; each time I gazed upon that moon-dead landscape and asked myself: what is out there? And each time I concluded: *something* is out there—maybe everything." What Billy learns as the story develops is that what is "out there" requires awareness, that it is difficult to define and that each man must see it for himself.

From the beginning of the story, Grandfather points out natural facts and repeatedly invites Billy to look. Tired of Lee's talk about the meaning of progress, Vogelin abruptly changes the subject: " 'Close your jaw and open your eyes and look at that mountain.' He raised an arm and pointed toward the granite of the high peak, now glowing with light from the rising sun." Billy, filled with a boy's questions, asks why they call it Thieves Mountain, but Grandfather does not give him an answer. Instead, he calls Billy's attention again to the mountain, as if it were a power in itself. "Look," he announces. "See how the light comes down the mountain now. Rolling toward us like a wave." And what Billy sees are sunlight images—intangibles—the sunlight spreading downward across the mountains and lower ridges covered with piñon and juniper. "Bands of light extended across the green sky, passing above us from the east, expanding from the fiery core that swelled below the rim of the world."

Later, Billy wants to see more and more. He insists that Lee tell him what he has seen on Thieves Mountain, but Lee turns the question back on Billy: "What do you see up there?" When Billy answers that he doesn't see anything, Lee keeps silent. After Billy persists: "There must be something up there," Lee asks him, "What are you looking for?" The question is the aware man's insistence that the boy see for himself the light on the land, the spirit of the natural world. But Billy remains puzzled, and Lee tells him that when he was on the mountain he had found only a little grass, some tiny flowers, wild sheep droppings, and an eagle's nest.

In the evening, camping at the line cabin, Billy at last sees the lion. Grandfather has sent him down to the spring for a bucket of water. He looks up toward a ledge and there stands the great beast. Billy is terrified. A minute later Grandfather comes looking for him, the big cat melts into darkness, and Vogelin, understanding the meaning of the event, puts his arm around the boy, leads the way back to the glow of the camp, and tells Lee what has happened. Recognizing the importance of this occasion, Lee smiles, "his deep eyes tender," grips Billy's arm, then offers him a cup of Grandfather's coffee. After the men have turned in, Billy lies awake listening to the horses and watching a meteor shoot across the sky. He understands now the relationship between the lion, the sunlight images, the "flaming blue stars," the meteor's soft light, and whatever the mountain top holds. It is something utterly intangible but immensely powerful, yet ever pulling back from the human touch. "Lee?" he asks.

"Up there on the peak: Was it—something like the lion?" When Lee agrees that it was, Billy thinks about that as he looks "straight up at the stars" which "became dimmer as I watched them, as if they were drifting farther and farther away from us. I closed my eyes," he says, "and slept and dreamed of the missing pony, fireflies, a pair of yellow eyes."

This is the kind of spiritual growth that Edward Abbey would urge upon all his readers. As a writer, he comes within the tradition proposed by Emerson. In his "American Scholar" address to Harvard's graduating class of 1837, Emerson defined the scholar, the writer, as an inspiring teacher of truths. "The office of the scholar," he announced, "is to cheer, to raise, and to guide men by showing them facts amidst appearances." Nature, Emerson believed, was the most important "of the influences upon the mind." The writer has a duty to understand and interpret nature, "the inexplicable continuity of this web of God," he called it. *Fire on the Mountain* attempts precisely that. How we shall *see* the land is the central question of the book. If we condemn vast sweeps of it for the inappropriate uses of a technological society, what does that condemnation mean for the rights of an old man like John Vogelin, for the mental and emotional health of a Lee Mackie, for the spiritual vision of a maturing boy like Billy? What does it mean for all of us and, ultimately, for nature itself? The answers to these hard questions, Abbey would like to suggest in this very well written little novel, are some of the most essential "facts amidst appearances" of our time.

The Carson Productions Interview

On November 23, 1981, NBC premiered the television version of Edward Abbey's novel, *Fire on the Mountain*, with a teleplay by John Sacret Young. The teleplay starred Buddy Ebsen as Vogelin and Ron Howard as Mackie. The film aired again on July 6, 1984. However, prior to the first airing, the former Vice President of Development at Carson Productions, Charmaine Balian, wrote as follows to Abbey on the 13th of November:

Dear Mr. Abbey:

I have express mailed these questions to you with the hopes that you will respond as expeditiously as you comfortably can.

I know that some of these may sound a little pedantic, so use them if you choose as a starting place. Any possible way that you can slip this into the mail by Sunday at the latest would give me the opportunity to meet a Tuesday deadline.

As a side note, because I was not able to express by phone, I would like you to know how important *Fire on the Mountain* was and is to me. I became so obsessed with Vogelin and what he stood for that it transcended the story and became part of my motivation during the film making process. I was infected with his spirit or maybe I began to get a better understanding of my deep sense of commitment to my values. Thank you very much for this beautiful man.

I can't promise you that the television movie will give you pleasure. But please know the effort was honest and filled with passion.

Abbey sent the following written responses to Balian's written questions:

BALIAN: How does *Fire on the Mountain*, written twenty years ago, nevertheless remain topical?

ABBEY: *Fire on the Mountain* deals with what I regard as the central conflict of the 20th Century: namely, the efforts of individuals, families and communities to preserve their freedom and integrity against the overwhelming power of the modern techno-industrial military superstate, here in America, in Europe, Asia, Africa, everywhere.

BALIAN: While the MX is different in size and shape from the "mobile missile" you describe in the book, the issue is obviously similar. Please comment.

ABBEY: The MX is merely the latest of many steps in the steady, gradual consolidation of military-industrial power in the U.S.A. It will probably never be used against our enemies abroad; indeed, within a decade or two it will be regarded as obsolete; but meanwhile our own people will be victimized by this vicious embezzlement of human material resources.

BALIAN: *Fire on the Mountain* stems from a real incident. Can you talk about that?

ABBEY: An actual New Mexico rancher, John Prather, was deprived of his home and property by the expansion of the missile-testing base at White Sands, New Mexico. This happened back in the mid-'50s. The old man died a few years later—of rage and heartbreak, I suspect.

BALIAN: Isn't it true that such incidents continue?

ABBEY: It is true that people continue to be driven out of their homes by various forms of industrial expansionism. For instance, the newly approved Tellico Dam in turn has destroyed the habitat not only of the famous little fish known as snail darter but also forced 341 farm families off their land. Most of them had lived and worked there for generations. Almost every time a new highway, power plant, military base, or research laboratory is established, we may safely assume that more wildlife, more people, more families will be forced to relocate.

BALIAN: Can you say something about the kind of man John Vogelin is?

ABBEY: I think the book describes him adequately: he is a personification of the traditional American ideal: an independent but neighborly guy, self-reliant and also kind, humorous, modest—a good man doing real work for an honest purpose.

BALIAN: A number of characters and names reoccur in your books—DeSalius, Burns and Hayduke, for example. Is this chance or design? If design, how so?

ABBEY: It began as chance but becomes a design following the evolutionary principle.

BALIAN: In a larger sense your books as a whole share a story. Not a single, simple story, but concerns and themes. They are relevant to *Fire on the Mountain*. Can you talk about them? What most is at the heart of your writing?

ABBEY: Figure it out.

BALIAN: Other authors—Wallace Stegner and Thomas McGuane—come to mind. They think greatly of your work. What about the other way around?

ABBEY: Among contemporary American authors there are many I respect and admire—McGuane, Nichols, Stegner, Eastlake, McMurtry, Houston, McDonnell, Graves, to name some fellow Westerners. There are many more fine writers among us—Gaddis, Pynchon, Coover, Stone, Doctorow, Heller, Vonnegut, Kotzwinkle, Berger—to name the ones I consider outstanding. America has produced a marvelous variety of literary artists in the last 35 years. I predict some of these people will be read and enjoyed long after the last of the authors of the moon-shots and Three-Mile Island are dead & buried & forgotten forever.

BALIAN: You don't own a television. Is it one of the things that doesn't qualify for John Vogelin's definition of progress of the modern man, like the disposable toothbrush?

ABBEY: True, we do not own a TV. We do not own a microwave oven. We do not own a 4 x 4 truck or a lawnmower or a motorboat or a trailbike or a home computer. We plan soon to be moving deeper into the country. I think we'll leave the telephone behind.

Barry Lopez

Meeting Ed Abbey

I first met Ed Abbey in Salt Lake City. We'd each been invited separately to the University of Utah to speak. He was kind enough to ask if I'd like to join him, to merge our dates in a benefit reading for the Utah Wilderness Association. I told him I'd be honored.

The hours before the reading were chaotic. Each of us spoke to separate groups of people. We lunched and then dined with faculty and students. We didn't have a chance to talk for more than a few minutes. But my impression of him hardly changed after that. He seemed both serene and startled in our moments together. There was something vital in him. I liked him immediately.

Writers, of course, are exceedingly diverse, and perhaps more wary around each other on first meeting than most, when they are put together by someone else in a public situation. The public persona each maintains to protect his privacy can make a wall between them, and distort what they might otherwise easily share. Too, one writer might believe the other is simply a drummer of some kind, and no writer.

67

The first words Ed and I had that night were about privacy. We were eating dinner. I said something about the vulnerability a reader can exhibit in a letter, and how respectful and careful I thought you had to be with such feelings. I was looking for a point of agreement. There is little enough time in life given to any of us; if your work is essentially private, it is better to locate the floor of an honest friendship quickly than to either proselytize or cajole with someone newly met, to assume agreements are there which are not. Writers, in my experience, can be courteous toward each other to a fault, especially in private; but they inhabit different and private universes, and the will to remain in them is iron. No friendship persists that requires one or the other to always defer, or which does not continue on a basis of mutual regard.

Readers bring writers together in curious ways. To some extent, writers are the creations of the shorthanded imagery of newspapers, of literary gossip. They are grouped regionally, placed in various "schools," or presumed to be somewhat like each other because they write about similar things. But writers maintain only tenuous friendships on these grounds—or become estranged because someone of note has glibly put them together, or separated them. Writers do not become friends solely because they write about the same things, nor solely because they admire each other's prose. They have to like each other as people, often as the people readers rarely know, because no writer can stand that kind of intimacy with readers and go on writing.

Ed was about to take a bite of his dinner when I said I thought you had to be respectful of vulnerability in readers. He paused with his fork in the air, and said yes, from somewhere far away in himself. The two of us, private men, both somewhat shy, found ourselves looking silently into the same abyss, and acknowledging a similar vulnerability in ourselves. A cynical remark at that moment and we would have forever gone our separate ways. But there was none. It was a moment of trust.

Writers, especially when they are possessed of some strong sense of their own worth and work—which is not always— are inclined compassionately toward each other. Each knows the other has struggled to make sense of that vast interior landscape of impressions, overheard conversations, sensual memories, feelings of longing and anguish, remembered sentences, and that wilderness of ethical rage and hope that creates literature. Only discipline and an abiding hunger produce fine work. And if another writer has produced fine work— you may not be stunned by its language, or agree with its sentiment, or even be keenly interested in its subject—you are moved. You know he has vanquished a nameless creature, a dreary beast that breaks tenacity, undermines faith, and leaves in its wake a convoluted prose. You know the same animal.

In those first moments with Ed I was struck by what I admire most in anyone: honesty; unpretentious convictions; a bedrock opposition to what menaces life. I imagined we might share enemies, though I felt no inclination to enumerate or describe them.

We read that evening together. The stories we read, about men and women in unmanipulated Western landscapes, expressed sentiments closely shared with people in the audience. I felt that night, strongly, almost physically, the beliefs I have about language—its power to evoke life and to remove pain—and the obligation writers have to dismantle the false notion of their own prophesies, the unexamined prejudices that can compel a public figure to demagoguery. I spoke that evening of a Spanish concept—*querencia*, a common, defended ground, an emotional landscape shared by listener and storyteller. Its defense implies a threat; without threat, without menace, there is neither literature nor heroism.

Abbey, with his caustic accusations and droll humor, his Western skepticism, was an encouragement to stand up for belief. As I listened to him read, I thought, well, here is a good man, a fine and decent neighbor. He reads before university audiences like this, is misunderstood, misquoted, misappropriated, but he goes on writing—an endless penetration of his own mind, a hunger for greater clarity, precision. How better this than were he to turn to politics, or to take solemnly the notion that he speaks for anyone but himself.

Since that evening I have gotten to know Ed better. The large and slow pleasure he takes in looking over the contours of a landscape, his affinity for music. A characteristic broad, sudden, and uncalculated smile. His ingenuous shyness, so at odds with the public image of a bold iconoclast.

We have specific disagreements, he and I, which we do not pursue, out of courtesy and a simple awareness of the frailty of human life, the gulf between human intent and human act. But nothing much has changed between us since that night, except that we have grown closer out of mutual regard, some unspoken sense of an opposition to a threat, a definition of which we largely agree upon.

You can point to the quirks and miscalculations of any writer exposed to the searing heat of public acclaim. Better to select what is admirable and encouraging, if a man is not a charlatan. Abbey's self-effacing honesty, the ease with which he can admire someone else's work without feeling he diminishes his own—these are qualities wonderful to find in any human. How fortunate for all of us that they are found in a man widely known and well regarded, who persists in writing out his understanding of the world as though it mattered to more than only himself.

70

Richard Shelton

Creeping Up on Desert Solitaire

I

Edward Abbey's *Desert Solitaire* has been hailed by critics as "an underground classic." Does this mean that the book was prematurely buried and will never rise from the grave? It seems an odd way to describe a book so filled with sky and sun, endless vistas, and soaring birds. In fact, *Desert Solitaire* is about the least "underground" book I have ever read. But it might be a "classic," whatever that is. Many literary "classics" have been hailed in the past, only to be lost sight of by the next generation of readers. Perhaps these books went underground, to the place, it would seem, where *Desert Solitaire* was born.

At any rate, few books in modern times can legitimately be called "classics" because few survive from one generation of readers to the next. And the term is becoming increasingly meaningless since we live in a time when we are not even sure there will be a next generation. And if there is a next generation which grows to maturity, will its members be readers in our sense of the word, or will they deal only with computerese and images on a television screen?

We know from medical statistics that a large percentage of the present generation of beautiful young people will be at least partially deaf and partially crippled by the time they reach middle age, one affliction caused by a penchant for extremely loud noise called "music," and the other by the current fad for jogging, which ultimately damages knees and ankles. What will these poor deaf cripples do when they are middle-aged, since their hearing impairments will limit the pleasure of television and they won't be able to move about much on their damaged legs? Perhaps they will revive reading as a pastime. Perhaps they will dig up old "underground classics" and read them. It might become a fad, and they could do worse.

But what will they think of Edward Abbey's *Desert Solitaire* when they finally get it exhumed? Lord, I don't know, and I don't want to know. The only way I can approach such a contemporary book critically is to creep up on it from behind, from the past into which it is rapidly receding. I cannot suggest that it will survive beyond the present generation of readers any more than I can suggest that the deserts and other beautiful places in this country will survive the forces of progress and tourism. I can hope, but hope is cheap and there is little of it in *Desert Solitaire*. Nor is it the stuff of serious literary criticism.

II

"Serious critics, serious librarians, serious associate professors of English will if they read this work dislike it intensely; at least I hope so," says Abbey in his "Author's Introduction" to *Desert Solitaire*. I was an associate professor of English when I first read *Desert Solitaire* and, with the exception of this patronizing sentence, I liked it intensely.

In fact, we associate professor types ate it up, as did our fusty friends the librarians. And it is a matter of record that most of the critics gave it high praise. Perhaps none of us were "serious" enough. But we have been loyal in praising the book and recommending it to everyone. Some of us have even taught it in our literature classes, heaven forbid! And Abbey, who is now a lecturer of English himself, does not seem to have been too displeased with our response to the book. Looking back, his statement seems to be part of a romantic "young rebel" pose based upon faulty assumptions and generalizations. But perhaps it was not merely a pose. Perhaps Abbey was trying to hide his love letters behind a smoke screen of abrasive rhetoric.

Obviously he wanted the book to be abrasive and con-troversial. At times he thunders like an Old Testament prophet denouncing the sins of a doomed people. At times he turns to ridicule with the flair, if not the subtlety, of an eighteenth-century satirist. But somehow or other those parts of the book went over our heads. As a matter of fact, we didn't use our heads much at all when we read *Desert Solitaire*. We fell in love with it. We took it directly into our hearts, however unused those dessicated organs were to such reac-tions. It became known as a sensuous, romantic masterpiece— exactly what its author, presumably, did not want it to be. Late in the book Abbey refers to "that gallant infirmity of the soul called romance—that illness, that disease, the insid-ious malignancy which must be chopped out of the heart once and for all, ground up, cooked, burnt to ashes . . . consumed."

Desert Solitaire was written by an arch-romantic trying des-perately not to be romantic. But between the realist who sees the hopeless condition of contemporary society with its hideous impact on nature and the lyric lover who wants only to sing about the beauties of the natural world "falls the shadow," as Mr. Eliot said; and Mr. Eliot had similar problems himself. That shadow is an unresolvable tension, the hope of the hopelessly romantic impulse faced with the inevitability of disaster. Out of such tension comes art, and perhaps without it there can be no art. This battle between two opposing impulses gives the book tension, drama, the shock of the real, and saves it from being just another memoir. Much of *Desert Solitaire* is a love lyric. But each time the lover gives in to romantic outpourings, the realist asserts himself, kills a rabbit or denounces, categorically, the shallowness, greed, and hypocrisy of man.

A reviewer for the *New York Times* called the book "a ride on a bucking bronco," and I can see what he means but would quarrel, somewhat, with the analogy. It is true that the book is all up and down, but the distances Abbey covers in both directions are infinitely greater than those experienced by anyone on a bucking horse. Stylistically and aesthetically the book rises to grand peaks of romantic beauty only to plunge suddenly downward with terrifying speed. And this pattern is often reflected in the physical actions described. Abbey is always climbing mountains or going to high places where his romantic spirit is nourished by the immensity of space and distance. Then he descends precipitously, almost in panic, from the place of too much beauty. He climbs Mt. Tukuhnikivats, the "island in the desert," grows lyrical at its summit, and then descends at a "sensational clip" by riding a slab of stone down the abrupt, snow-covered side of the mountain.

But he likes best to stand on the edge of a cliff or at the summit of a very high place and watch the birds, often buzzards, soaring without effort through the sea of space below. The descent beckons. He feels the lure of high places and the desire to launch himself into space like Rilke looking out from the balcony of a romantic castle tower above the Rhine. He even quotes Rilke with respect and then, with that sudden turning away from the romantic, describes him as "a German poet who lived off countesses." In the chapter called "The Dead Man at Grandview Point" Abbey creates a symbol of the earthbound, pedestrian man who allows himself to die of thirst and exposure at the edge of a cliff rather than take the romantic plunge, after which his body would become part of the soaring birds rather than a stinking mess of putrefaction zipped up in a rubber bag, a burden for those who must carry it miles toward a waiting ambulance and further indignities.

One of the results of this tension, this attraction of opposites—the soaring romantic and the cynically realistic, high places and the sudden descent—is that Abbey, as he portrays himself in the book, is a round and believable character. No character in any of his novels has the depth, the believability, the absolute feel of a real person that Ed Abbey in *Desert Solitaire* has. Compared to Ed Abbey in *Desert Solitaire, The Brave Cowboy* or anybody in *The Monkey Wrench Gang* or *Good News* is flat and dimensionless. But this man, this Ed Abbey who can fall in love with a weathered juniper and then coolly consider beating a companion's brains out with a beer bottle, this man is real.

At times he is complex, deep, philosophical, and wise. At other times he is shallow, cynical, or cruel; and he visits most of the way stations between. Whether he is the Edward Abbey who wrote the book or that Edward Abbey's view of himself or a purely fictional creation is a matter of little importance, except perhaps to the youthful members of the cult which has grown up around the book, those who are sometimes puzzled and possibly a bit disappointed by the tall, soft-spoken, shy, and reticent man named Edward Abbey whom they travel hundreds of miles to meet.

Whoever he is, the Ed Abbey in *Desert Solitaire* is human, and he works. He works the way a character in fiction should work. He has weight, stature, variety. He poses and postures, makes fun of himself and others, takes himself seriously, is loving and hateful, strong and weak by turns. And he is created right on the spot, full-blown, with almost no anterior personality and only the most minimal explanation as to how he got there or how he got to be who he is.

In the "Author's Introduction" Abbey tells the reader that he spent three summers as a park ranger at Arches National Monument in southeast Utah. The "Author's Introduction" is brief, and much of what it says deals with the National Park Service and with Abbey's method of writing the book. He says, ". . . most of the substance of this book is drawn, sometimes direct and unchanged, from the pages of journals I kept. . . ." If the date and place of its signing can be trusted, the "Author's Introduction" was written in Nelson's Marine Bar in Hoboken in April, 1967, after the book was completed. But it does not seem to have been written by the Ed Abbey who is the narrator and point-of-view character in the book. That Ed Abbey appears quite suddenly on page one. The first thing he says is, "This is the most beautiful place on earth." And he's not referring to Nelson's Marine Bar in Hoboken.

The line between fiction and nonfiction, between storytelling and reportage or writing essays, has always been tenuous. If it seems to be growing more tenuous lately with the nonfiction novels of Truman Capote and Norman Mailer, that is only because we have a shortsighted view. There was once a Daniel Defoe, and before him a Thomas Nash, a Robert Greene, and others. We have come to accept the principle that novelists make up stories and writers of nonfiction do not, but that is a recent convention and will not hold up to historical facts. It seems to me that if the literary output of Edward Abbey, as a whole, should be compared to that of some illustrious writer of the past, that writer would probably be Daniel Defoe. I am not prepared to pursue this and feel intimidated even by bringing it up, but perhaps someone better equipped to do so might want to consider it at length.

Certainly some sections of *Desert Solitaire* are short stories, some are tales, some are vignettes, some are narrative reports based on journal notes. In some sections the author treats plot, character, and dialogue exactly as a short story writer would treat them. In other sections he uses the essayist's means to convince the reader in regard to philosophical issues.

What holds these disparate structural elements together? Perhaps it is not even legitimate to ask such a question this late in the twentieth century. Perhaps unity or structural integrity is no longer an element we can expect in a book. But I feel a strong, almost desperate, attempt on the author's part to make this book hang together, to make it a unit rather than a hodgepodge of essays, narratives, and short stories. And for me he succeeds, although if I had been given an outline of the book before it was written, I would probably have said it couldn't be done. But *Desert Solitaire* is a *tour de force*, and such works, by definition, must succeed in spite of severe technical obstacles.

Since there is little unity of subject or structure, Abbey tries to rely on the unities of time and place to make the book cohere. He compresses the events of three seasons in the wilderness into one season, and he generally limits himself to a loosely defined geographical area, although that area is quite literally as big as all outdoors. Sometimes he violates one or both of these limitations, narrating events which took place at an earlier period or in a somewhat different place, such as the story of the ill-fated uranium prospector Albert T. Husk or the account of Abbey's sojourn in Havasu Canyon. But the stories are fascinating, and most readers are not all that familiar with the geography anyway. After all, it is a remote area in a godforsaken corner of Utah.

There are, however, several things which recur in the book much like *leitmotifs*. Somehow, we are more accustomed to such devices in poetry or the novel, and it is easy to miss their structural and unifying functions in a work of nonfiction. The lone juniper, the red bandana, the trailer, the natural stone terrace, the outdoor fire—to these Abbey returns the reader again and again. They define a space which is the center of the book, the place where Abbey sleeps, eats and meditates on the desert. Near the center of that space is the fire, a small circle of light which gives the book a *locus* around which to circulate.

It would seem easy to say that *Desert Solitaire* has a unity of subject because, as its name implies, it is a book about the desert; and there might be some truth in this, but it is also misleading. There are many books which we would all agree were written about the desert, but they were written by scientists like Paul Griswold Howes, Forrest Shreve, or William McGinnies, or by historians like Eugene Hollow. Some of these are fairly heavy going for a nonspecialist, but they are clearly *about* the desert. Others, easier to read but still filled with factual information, were written by amateur naturalists like Joseph Wood Krutch. Is *Desert Solitaire* about the desert?

We need not quibble over this. Let us go straight to the horse's mouth, keeping in mind that even the horse can

sometimes be wrong or misleading. In his "Author's Introduction" Abbey says:

> This is not primarily a book about the desert. In
> recording my impressions of the natural scene I have
> striven above all for accuracy, since I believe that there
> is a kind of poetry, even a kind of truth, in simple fact.
> But the desert is a vast world, an oceanic world, as deep
> in its way and complex and various as the sea. Lan-
> guage makes a mighty loose net with which to go
> fishing for simple facts, when facts are infinite. . . .
> What I have tried to do then is something a bit differ-
> ent. Since you cannot get the desert into a book any
> more than a fisherman can haul up the sea with his
> nets, I have tried to create a world of words in which
> the desert figures more as a medium than as a mate-
> rial. Not imitation but evocation has been the goal.

I am primarily interested in three words here: "impressions," "medium," and "evocation." This could be the language of an impressionist painter or of a romantic poet. Yet
the book is obviously neither a painting nor a poem. If the
desert is a "medium" for something, what is it a "medium"
for? And if "evocation" is Abbey's goal, what is he trying
to evoke? There may not be definitive answers to these questions, but they are important questions nonetheless, since
they lead to a central issue. If *Desert Solitaire* is not primarily
about the desert, what is it about? And does it have any clear
literary antecedents or models, or is it merely a twentieth-
century anomaly?

The fact that Abbey talks about the book in terms one
might use to describe a poem is a little frightening. Is it written in that abomination called "poetic prose"? I certainly
hope not, and a close look at the language assures me that it

is not. Even at his most rhapsodic, and Abbey does rhapso-
dize from time to time, the language is crisp, muscular, idi-
omatic, and concrete. There is an orderliness and clarity
about his prose which suggests French models. His writing
is never muddy nor self-indulgent, and if he sometimes flirts
with "purple passages," they are only faintly lilac. The lyrical quality of *Desert Solitaire* arises from what Abbey is saying
rather than from the way he says it. It comes from his atti-
tude toward what he is writing about.

As for literary models, toward the end of the book Abbey
provides a brief, handy-dandy list of books written about
or in response to the desert. All of them have at least interested him, and some of them might have influenced him.
In some cases he mentions only authors, but it is obvious
which books he is referring to, and a mixed bag it is.

It includes four books (by John Wesley Powell, Everett
Ruess, Charles M. Doughty, and T.E. Lawrence) which fall
clearly into the category of travel and exploration, as well
as two books by Wallace Stegner, one a biography and one
a history. It refers, but not by title, to some of the novels of
Paul Bowles and William Eastlake. The remaining three
books are collections of essays. They include a book of
essays on the Sonoran Desert by Joseph Wood Krutch, and
a collection by Mary Austin, whose interests ranged from
natural history to anthropology. The remaining book is un-
classifiable. It might be considered a travel book, but it isn't.
It might be considered a collection of essays on natural history, but it isn't. It is John Charles Van Dyke's turn-of-the-
century masterpiece, *The Desert*, which Abbey refers to as
"an unjustly forgotten book."

Of all the books on Abbey's list, *The Desert* has the strongest claim of being the direct literary antecedent of that part
of *Desert Solitaire* which is presented in essay form. In 1901,
in his "Preface-Dedication" to *The Desert* Van Dyke said:

The love of Nature is after all an acquired taste. One begins by admiring the Hudson-River landscape and ends by loving the desolation of Sahara. Just why or how the change would be difficult to explain. You cannot always dissect a taste or a passion. Nor can you pin Nature to a board and chart her beauties with square and compasses. One can give his impression and but little more. Perhaps I can tell you something of what I have seen in these two years of wandering; but I shall never be able to tell you the grandeur of these mountains, nor the glory of the color that wraps the burning sands at their feet. We shoot arrows at the sun in vain; yet still we shoot.

If we compare this passage with the passage from Abbey's "Author's Introduction" previously quoted, it becomes apparent that the two men are saying remarkably similar things. And in spite of the differences in prose styles which reflect the styles of two different periods, both express themselves in remarkably similar ways. Both use the term "impression," and both turn to metaphor to express the impossibility of a factual approach to their subject. But what, exactly, is their subject? Abbey talks about hauling up the entire sea in a net, and Van Dyke describes what he is doing as shooting arrows at the sun. They are both evasive, and thereby hangs a tale.

III

The Desert by John Charles Van Dyke is a remarkable book not only because of what it is, but also because of what it is not. Although it is filled with precise observations, it does not provide the reader with the kind of facts provided by

Joseph Wood Krutch's *The Desert Year*. And it is not a travel book, although its author had surely traveled. He was a handsome, asthmatic, forty-two-year-old art critic and art historian who wandered through the desert of the southwestern United States and northwestern Mexico for more than two years, sometimes on horseback and sometimes on foot. The subtitle of his book is *Further Studies in Natural Appearances*, and Van Dyke claims that it is a careful record of what he observed during his wanderings. But one of the strange things about it is that Van Dyke almost never tells the reader where he was while making particular observations, and much of the time the reader has no idea which of three different deserts Van Dyke was looking at.

In spite of that, Van Dyke had a pair of the best-trained eyes of his generation. He had spent much of his life looking at paintings and writing about paintings, aesthetics, and theories of visual perception. He was also a professor of art history at Rutgers University, and he was in love with the desert. His high degree of perceptual training combined with his extreme emotional involvement resulted in a book which glows from within.

He organizes his observations thematically in chapters with such titles as "Light, Air, and Color" or "Illusions." He describes and analyzes with the precision of a scientist and even performs simple scientific experiments to obtain more accurate information, but he writes from the standpoint of a lover. The desert holds him; and it holds him in spite of ill health, danger, deprivation, loneliness, and depression. Caught in the tension between the impulses of a scientist or scholar and those of a lover, he tries desperately to express his obsession:

> . . . you shall never see elsewhere as here the sunset valleys swimming in a pink and lilac haze, the great mesas and plateaus fading into blue distance, the gorges and canyons banked full of purple shadow. . . . And wherever you go, by land or sea, you shall not forget what you saw not but rather felt—the desolation and the silence of the desert.

A comparison of specific passages in *The Desert* and *Desert Solitaire* would provide evidence of nothing as startling as literary "borrowing," but it would provide interesting results. It would show two men with the same obsession, both in love with the same landscape. That landscape is a hard mistress and not the mistress of their choice, but neither of them had a choice. They had significantly different backgrounds and are writing more than sixty years apart. Their prose styles are quite different, but their music is the same, as each tries to come to grips with his own feelings.

"What is the peculiar quality or character of the desert that distinguishes it, in spiritual appeal, from other forms of landscape?" Abbey asks, as if he believes he could really answer the question, although he knows Van Dyke has already tried to answer it and failed. Van Dyke's version was: "What is it that draws us to the boundless and fathomless? Why should the lovely things of the earth . . . appear trivial and insignificant when we come face to face with . . . the desert?"

When Abbey speaks of being "caught by this golden lure," I think we begin to see what both of these books are about, and why neither of them falls neatly into any literary category. These books compare to most books about the desert as the description of a beautiful woman written by her lover would compare to a description of the same woman written by her physician. The physician's description might be more accurate; but the lover's description would go well beyond the physical, would involve the emotional and spiritual, and would undoubtedly be colored by how the woman had treated him. Abbey says, "I am convinced now that the desert has no heart." He is speaking as a man in love, as Van Dyke spoke before him.

The account of Abbey's leave-taking of Arches National Monument in *Desert Solitaire* could easily be the description of a man parting from a woman with whom he is deeply in love, a woman he does not think he will ever see again. To use an old cliché, but one for which no adequate substitute has yet been found, it is heartbreaking: the preparations for departure; the long, sensuous lingering over every physical detail of the beloved; the awkward and sentimental gestures; then the need to be gone quickly while he still has the strength; and finally, while he is being driven away and it is too late, the desperate looking back. It has been done before in literature, and perhaps it is a stock scene; but it has never been done before, not even by Van Dyke, with a desert.

Van Dyke, in his "Preface-Dedication" says: "The desert has gone a-begging for a word of praise these many years. It never had a sacred poet; it has in me only a lover." Earlier in the same paragraph he says, "And so my book is only an excuse for talking about the beautiful things in this desert world. . . ." And perhaps that is a good enough answer to the question of what both *Desert Solitaire* and *The Desert* are about. Neither writer needs much excuse to talk about the beauty of his beloved; nor, for that matter, do any of us. The French have a name for such a thing when it is a poem. They call it a *blazon*, a catalogue of the beauty of the beloved. But we have no such category in English prose, and therefore both books remain quite without category, not an entirely undesirable place for a literary work to be.

Both Van Dyke and Abbey, while they were in the desert, were aware of its numinous quality, of some spirit which it contains or embodies. Van Dyke speaks of the desert's "soul," and Abbey speaks of its "heart." Both were frustrated, but their attempts to find it led them far beyond what most writers have been able to achieve when dealing with the desert. Their search led them into the realms of the mystic or transcendental. Van Dyke's attempt, since it involved longer periods of total isolation, more danger, solitude, and deprivation, was probably greater. As he admits in his unpublished Autobiography, it destroyed his health and led him to the brink of madness. In *The Desert* he says:

> Was there ever such stillness as that which rests upon the desert at night? Was there ever such a hush as that which steals from star to star across the firmament? You perhaps think to break that spell by raising your voice in a cry; but you will not do so again. The sound goes but a little way and then seems to come back to your ear with a suggestion of insanity about it.

And Abbey provides a daytime version of the same mystery:

> There is something about the desert that the human sensibility cannot assimilate, or has not so far been able to assimilate. Perhaps that is why it has scarcely been approached in poetry or fiction, music or painting. . . . Meanwhile, under the vulture-haunted sky, the desert waits—mesa, butte, canyon, reef, sink, escarpment, pinnacle, maze, dry lake, sand dune and barren mountain—untouched by the human mind.

Since both Van Dyke and Abbey were in love with the desert, their books have another element in common—a plea for its protection. And because of what happened to much of the desert of the southwestern United States in the more than sixty years since Van Dyke wrote *The Desert*, Abbey's book is more bitter, more pessimistic, more despairing; and this in spite of the fact that Van Dyke refers to man as nature's "one great enemy," and says, "The desert should never be reclaimed." After he wrote that, Van Dyke lived to see much of the Colorado and Mojave deserts destroyed by reclamation projects, and he witnessed the disastrous attempt to divert part of the Colorado River which created the Salton Sea.

But he did not see the worst, the horrors of progress: the destruction of large portions of the Sonoran Desert by agriculture, desert cities spreading like cancer, the further rape of the Colorado River to provide power to air-condition the tract houses and shopping malls of Phoenix. Abbey writes with a full knowledge of these horrors, and if his irony sometimes turns to bitterness, his bitterness is justified by what he has seen.

Abbey's employment as a park ranger, even in so remote a place as Arches National Monument, put him in an excellent position to view the American middle class in its tourist phase, with its penchant for litter, conveniences, and the automobile. His description of the American tourist is savagely accurate. He pinpoints the automobile as the immediate cause of the destruction of the natural environments which are supposed to be protected by the National Park Service, and blames that organization for encouraging the destruction of the very thing it is supposed to be protecting.

Nor is Abbey always negative. He proposes specific methods for "carving some of the fat off the wide bottom of the American middle class," and he outlines in detail a very sensible method for saving our national parks while still making them available to the people. One has only to go to Arches or Mesa Verde or any of the other national parks or monuments today to see that the governmental forces which control them have paid not the slightest attention to what he said.

It is probably because of Abbey's stand on environmental issues that *Desert Solitaire* has been tagged an *"underground* classic." I object to the use of the term "underground," since it suggests somehow that the book is subversive and makes it easier to dismiss Abbey's ideas and recommendations. But I see nothing subversive about *Desert Solitaire*. Abbey's very specific suggestions are aimed at conserving, not destroying. And if, when he makes them, his tone at times is somewhat strident and abrasive, beneath it I always hear the voice of a lover trying desperately to protect the thing he loves. It is a strong, clear voice. The pity is there are not more voices like it.

Dave Solheim and Rob Levin

The *Bloomsbury Review* Interview

Dave Solheim and Rob Levin conducted the following composite interview with Edward Abbey. It first appeared in the November/December 1980 issue of *The Bloomsbury Review*, a bold, bimonthly magazine devoted to writers and books with justifiable emphasis on the American West. At the time of the interview, Dave Solheim was a graduate student in creative writing at the University of Denver, Rob Levin a reporter for *The Arizona Daily Star*. Solheim and Levin prefaced their interview with the two paragraphs below:

"Probably more than any other living writer, Edward Abbey is the spokesman for the American West. He has published six novels (the most recent of which, *Good News*, is reviewed in this issue) and eight books of non-fiction essays and travelogues. Although he is one of the leading spokesmen for the preservation of wilderness, he defies labels. He believes in wilderness first of all for its own sake, and secondly because it allows human beings to have feelings of danger and freedom which are too often removed from modern life. He is not the new Thoreau of anything, but will wear, if somewhat uncomfortably, the labels of anarchist

89

and wild preservationist. But don't let that fool you. Abbey is as diverse and slippery as the slickrock country he writes about and as predictable as a flashflood.

"Abbey lives at home in the desert southwest near Tucson with his wife and two dogs, Bones and Elly. The dogs are like him in that they prefer to spend the day wandering the desert. His clothing frequently looks government issued, maybe left over from his previous work as a park ranger, forest ranger, and fire lookout. He wears combat boots made in Taiwan. 'They feel good; they wear well.' Though he may at first appear as a slightly disheveled Smokey the Bear, Abbey is far from G.I. He is consistently radical, but relishes the complications and contradictions of being human."

THE BLOOMSBURY REVIEW: In some of your novels, major characters seem to be killed only to return to life later: Jack Burns in *The Brave Cowboy* and in *Good News*, and George Hayduke in *The Monkey Wrench Gang*. Are you too attached to your characters to finally kill them off, or is there more justification for these resurrections than I have noticed?

EDWARD ABBEY: I believe in happy endings, and furthermore, I do not understand my own books, very well, anyway. Jack Burns also appears in *The Monkey Wrench Gang*. I do like to keep my endings open. The first edition of *The Brave Cowboy* was too closed, but I corrected that in the later editions.

BLOOMSBURY: Can your readers expect to hear more of Hayduke or Burns in future novels?

ABBEY: Very likely.

BLOOMSBURY: Maybe the middle of Jack Burns's life?

ABBEY: That's a good idea.

BLOOMSBURY: George Hayduke seems to be a sociopath. He wants to drive his jeep and throw his empty beer cans wherever he wants to. Is even the West big enough for more than one or two Haydukes? Do you have any reservations about presenting such a character in a favorable light?

ABBEY: Hayduke is Hayduke. I do not feel responsible for his behavior.

BLOOMSBURY: *The Monkey Wrench Gang* suggests that old four-wheel drives are good and that new ones deserve to have boulders dropped on them; that it's OK to use a chain saw on billboards, but not on trees. Is that important to the novel?

ABBEY: I think that I shall never see a billboard lovely as a tree.

BLOOMSBURY: At the end of *Desert Solitaire* you suggest that both the city and the wilderness are necessary for modern human existence. *Good News*, your latest novel, opens presenting "the oldest civil war, that between the city and the country." Does this show a change in your thinking or did your idea of balance include the tension of conflict or even war?

ABBEY: All of the above. I'd like to live fairly near a city, but I don't have any desire to live in a city. Where I'm at now suits me fine. If it'd stay this way, I could live here the rest of my life. But very likely, this will all be built up in a few years.

I'd like to live fifty or sixty miles out in the country from a city like Tucson or Santa Fe. Or Salt Lake. Or five hundred miles out in the country and get an airplane and a pilot's license.

As I've said before, I'm not a recluse or a hermit. I like some social life. I'd like to have the best of both worlds. The wilderness and urban civilization.

BLOOMSBURY: You are noted for the political-activist stance of your novels. Do you have to control your characters to serve your political ends?

ABBEY: I try to control my characters, but they almost always get out of hand. They like to go their own ways.

BLOOMSBURY: I have a half-baked theory that one distinguishing feature of western literature is that the landscape is an active character, a participant in the events of a novel; that the landscape acts on, and interacts with, the human characters. In *Good News* landscape is replaced by a burned-out cityscape. Is that important?

ABBEY: I certainly agree that the landscape is a major character in most western novels, and probably should be. But I also believe that the land acts upon and shapes human beings everywhere, eastern as well as western, city as well as country.

BLOOMSBURY: I guess that takes care of my theory.

ABBEY: I do think that you're right. The land, the earth of the American West, is unique. It acts in ways that are hard to describe.

BLOOMSBURY: In your introduction to *Abbey's Road*, you mention a number of writers whom you respect. You seem to be the only western writer I'm familiar with (except for Tom Robbins, whom you don't mention and might not be a western writer) who has an urbane, ironic wit in your work. Would you comment on that, or correct me where I'm wrong?

ABBEY: Well, I'm not a Tom Robbins fan. I like his first book, *Another Roadside Attraction*. I tried to read *Even Cowgirls Get the Blues* but could not get through it. It's just too cutesy-pie for me. I regard him as a kind of shampoo artist or a cotton-candy vendor. Writers whom I really admire who live in, or write about the West are: William

Eastlake, Wallace Stegner, Tom McGuane, Wright Morris, Larry McMurtry, and I think all of them have plenty of wit and irony.

BLOOMSBURY: Would you discuss a few of your favorite writers, both classic and contemporary, and tell why they are your favorites?

ABBEY: Well, I suppose it's much more interesting, isn't it, opinions on contemporary writers. We all admire Shakespeare and Tolstoy, or most of us do. There's nothing much new to say about them. Well, I like McGuane and Pynchon. Oh, Christ, I'm not much of a critic, I'm not very good at analyzing things. I think it's probably a matter of style. I just admire very much the way they write, the way they handle the language. Have you read Pynchon? *Gravity's Rainbow*? It's almost incomprehensible to me. I find great difficulty in what the hell he's saying as I go along, but I read it anyway. I enjoy it. I find it fascinating, even though it's so complex and dense and obscure and mysterious that I don't know quite what he's saying.

McGuane is a very clear writer, although he has opaque paragraphs here and there. His writing always has a kind of bloodchilling nihilism to it that I can't always find appealing. But it's interesting, it's powerful.

Another contemporary writer I admire would be William Eastlake, also a friend of mine. He lives down in Bisbee, a small town about ninety miles southeast of Tucson, on the border. He wrote some novels about life in New Mexico. He wasn't very serious about it. He wrote three novels about contemporary New Mexico. And they are marvelous novels. Indians and cowboys and jazz musicians and tourists and ranchers and written in a very witty, ironic style. Eastlake is also a master of the sentence and paragraph.

And there's Alan Harrington. I might as well put in another plug for a writer and friend who lives out here in Tucson. He, I think, is a great essayist. He wrote the book *The Immortalist*. *The Immortalist* is not a novel. It's a 300-page essay on the subject of death and immortality—the very things we were told to avoid as journalism students. It's a very interesting book, full of interesting ideas. And Alan has also written some good novels, mostly about New York life. He was a New Yorker for about twenty years. He moved out here about ten years ago. And he just finished a novel a few days ago called *The White Rainbow*, which is about Mexico and the old Aztec traditions, human sacrifice—kind of a morbid book, but very interesting. I've read parts of it and he's read parts of it to me.

I like Nabokov quite a lot. I was shocked that he did not get the Nobel Prize. I admire him chiefly as a stylist, a master of the language. He's a Russian who can write English much better than many of us Americans.

B. Traven is another literary hero of mine. He's not such a well-known American writer, if he was American. His whole life was sort of a mystery. He may have been born in Germany. He lived most of his life in Mexico. He wrote *The Treasure of Sierra Madre,* which became the famous movie. But he wrote about half a dozen other novels which are just as good. His best was one called *The Death Ship*, about a sailor's life in the merchant marines in the 1920s.

Well, I could go on and on. There are many living writers I admire. I think there's a helluva lot of challenge here in the United States. No writer that I would call great. I don't think we have another Faulkner among us. But who knows. Pynchon is still fairly young, and so is McGuane. I think they're both in their thirties.

BLOOMSBURY: At least for the last few years you have lived in the rural Southwest. How important is that location for your writing? Would you be as significant a writer as you are now if you had continued to live in New Jersey or New York?

ABBEY: That's a good way to phrase it. I sometimes suspect I might have been a better writer if I'd stayed back East; it's a lot easier to sit indoors there. But I don't think I'd be so happy a man. The Southwest is definitely my home, and I think it always will be. At least I hope so. I've lived here a long time. Since 1947 except for a year in Europe and one year in New York. So I've lived most of my life in the Southwest.

BLOOMSBURY: Is there one state or town that you consider home? You've said that you were going to leave here when your wife finished college. You've lived many other places. Does it make any difference so long as it's in the Southwest?

ABBEY: I call a very large area home. Parts of Mexico, Baja California, all the way up into parts of Wyoming. I don't think it matters very much. I really do regard the whole Southwest as my home. I'm perfectly happy to live anywhere in Arizona, New Mexico, Utah, Nevada. I like the desert; I like the hot, dry climate. I hate to be cold and wet, especially both at the same time.

BLOOMSBURY: You have said some harsh things about the New York publishing establishment. Your books have been published by large houses and reissued by the University of New Mexico Press. What role do you see that university presses, small presses, and non-commercial presses have in the world of publishing conglomerates?

ABBEY: I'm all for them. I think there will always be a role for the small presses and the university presses. They serve as outlets for scholarly work and for new and experimental fiction, and writing by new and unknown authors that the national publishers will not take a chance on. I think both of these presses are useful and necessary and always have been in American literature. You may recall that Thoreau paid for publication of his first book of which he sold two hundred copies out of a printing of two thousand. The advantage of big publishers is the large audience. A writer wants to be read by as many people as possible.

BLOOMSBURY: At this stage of your career, you probably have no need for it, but did you ever want to work in a community of writers? What do you think about university writing programs?

ABBEY: First of all, I don't have a career, only a life. Writing books is a passion. But it's only one of several passions. No, I would not want to work in a community of writers. Trying to live with one writer—myself—is difficult enough. Many other writers have influenced me, certainly. But they're not to blame for anything. As for college writing programs, I doubt if they do any harm.

If a student is interested in writing, or wants to become a writer, he probably should take a writing class. I took one or two when I was a student. They might teach you something, but most of all they give you pressure to write. That's the hardest thing about writing—to get started, to put the first things down on a page.

BLOOMSBURY: What makes you write now? When you've been loafing, hiking, hanging out for a year or so do you make notes on things? When do you decide you can't put it off any longer? Does the pressure to write keep building?

ABBEY: I do make notes. I have such a bad memory that I have to, or I'd forget everything.

There are two forms of pressure. One is psychological and the other is financial. I make my living by writing—mostly. I've also made a partial living from being a fire lookout.

You know, the psychological pressure builds up. If I'm not writing, I begin to feel guilty, useless. Sloth and bloat set in. I get itchy. I'm too much of a Puritan to be a good loafer, I guess. And also, I take assignments, do magazine articles, have to meet deadlines. . . .

BLOOMSBURY: In *Abbey's Road* you claim to wear a tie when you write. You aren't wearing one now.

ABBEY: I have worn a tie. I will probably die in one.

BLOOMSBURY: Several of your characters have spent time in jail. Have you?

ABBEY: Yes, I have been in jail a few times. Once for vagrancy, once for public drunkenness, once for reckless driving—what the police called "negligent driving"—rather trivial offenses. I'm not very proud of them. But I think it's important for a writer to spend at least one night in jail, maybe even more important for lawyers and judges. I have *not* been in jail for refusing to pay taxes. I tried to not pay taxes in the late sixties, but they just went to my employer at the time and garnished my wages.

BLOOMSBURY: Violence is in most of your writing. Has violence directly affected you in any way?

ABBEY: As for violence, I'm against it for I am a practical coward. However, violence is an integral part of the modern world, modern civilization, and I assume that someday I may have to face it. So I load my own ammo. There are a few things worth killing for. Not many, but a few.

BLOOMSBURY: Your master's thesis in philosophy was a study of the ethics of violence. I understand you were frustrated by restraints placed on it by the faculty committee?

97

ABBEY: Yes, I wanted to write a book that I was going to call the ":General Theory of Anarchism." Fortunately, the thesis committee was not interested in that kind of tome, or I'd still be working on that first treatise.

BLOOMSBURY: Although you've been reluctant to talk about it, when you were the editor of *The Thunderbird*, the student literary magazine at the University of New Mexico, the university president suspended its publication for a year.

ABBEY: Well, in my case it was kind of a showoff stunt. It was sort of silly, but what I did was put a quote on the cover of this magazine that said: "Mankind will never be free until the last king is strangled by the entrails of the last priest." And I attributed that to Louisa May Alcott. False, of course. It was some Frenchman. Diderot, I believe. And of course, I got the Catholics in an uproar about that. I don't blame them. It was kind of a stupid thing to do. I was just trying to attract attention.

BLOOMSBURY: You said you were a practical coward?

ABBEY: Well, I try to avoid direct physical violence if possible. I've never been in a barroom fight. I've been in plenty of barrooms. Some close calls, but usually, always, I've been able to talk my way out of it. I haven't been in a fight since about the fourth grade when I beat up my best friend, the only guy in the class I could lick.

BLOOMSBURY: How do you feel about your work being the subject of academic study? Would you prefer a barroom discussion of your books to a classroom discussion?

ABBEY: I don't care where my books are read or by whom. I'm happy to be read by anybody, anywhere. I've no objection to people talking about them in a classroom or a barroom, as long as it's done voluntarily by willing victims.

BLOOMSBURY: They could be required reading.

ABBEY: Well, no one is required to go to college. At least not yet.

BLOOMSBURY: You aren't worried about what academic people might do to your work?

ABBEY: No. I don't think about it. Let them do their work. I'll do mine.

BLOOMSBURY: After people read your books, how would you like them to think of you, or do you care?

ABBEY: All writers need love, appreciation. I think I write mainly to please myself, because that's the easiest way for me to write. I don't have any analytical or critical ability. I cannot design a book very well. I write rapidly, spontaneously, out of the belly and bowels. And usually from a very personal point of view.

Most of my work doesn't get very good reviews, especially back East. I've got this grudge against New York book reviewers. I don't think they take me seriously. All western writers feel this way, though. All of us who live out here and write out here.

As I said, we all want to be loved, appreciated. Fame. The desire for fame is certainly one of the motives for writing. I suppose there's a danger in too much fame, too much money. I guess that could spoil a writer. I haven't had an opportunity to deal with that yet. But I'm willing to take the chance.

I think all writers are egotists. I wasn't much good at athletics. I couldn't even make the high school basketball team. Oh, I suppose it's true that artistic ability in writing is compensation for failure in some other line. But I wouldn't make much of that.

I think writers have it pretty good. Especially anybody that can make a living by writing, which I've been able to do for the last ten years. I'm a pretty lucky person, which doesn't necessarily mean I'll be happy.

BLOOMSBURY: You present yourself and seem to think of yourself as a novelist. Suppose, for the sake of argument, that you are considered to be more important as an essayist, or worse yet, a nature writer. How would that affect you and your writing?

ABBEY: I go my own way, do the best I can, writing mainly to please myself. But it is on the assumption that there is an audience out there somewhere, made up of people pretty much like myself, or at least of people who think and feel like me. So far that approach seems to work. I don't know whether I'm primarily a novelist or essayist or something in between. I don't really worry about that.

BLOOMSBURY: What would you say are your strengths and weaknesses as a writer?

ABBEY: I guess I'd have to divide fiction from non-fiction to answer that question. As an essayist—I like to call myself an essayist, it sounds good, instead of a journalist. I've said some nasty things about journalism, journalists. But I'm a journalist myself half the time, when I do my magazine writing. I was once editor of a small-town weekly. For six months I was editor of the Taos weekly newspaper. It went out of business, and I lost my job. I took journalism in high school, flunked it twice. Same course, flunked it twice. I just couldn't get the facts straight. I had a hard time making the news fit the page, doing the layouts. So all those nasty remarks I made about journalists were meant to be, hopefully, a put-on. But I would like to call myself an essayist. But anyway, getting on to the weaknesses. . . .

On non-fiction, and I've been criticized for this, I tend to be self-indulgent. I ramble on and on. I write too much about myself. Sometimes it works pretty well, but it can be overdone. After a while, the reader gets really tired of hearing about the writer's personal problems and opinions. He'd like a more objective point of view, a description of what's going on out there.

In fiction, I've published six novels now, and I wrote a couple of more that were unpublished, rejected. And I've got two or three more in my head that I want to write. My main difficulty in fiction, especially in novel form, is plotting. How to arrange the material in the most effective way. I just don't understand how you construct a plot. I generally follow the obvious, most simple way. Beginning at the beginning, follow a linear chronology. I tried writing short stories long, long ago. I found them even more difficult. There you really have to exercise discipline, know what you're doing. I'm not any good at that. For me, the novel is easier to write than the short story. You can get away with more looseness and carelessness. I can't say any more. I don't like to talk about my weaknesses.

BLOOMSBURY: You already have. But what about your strengths?

ABBEY: Oh, hell, I can't analyze my own work. I really just write to suit myself. I work very fast, in spasms and in spurts and loaf a lot between projects, books or articles. I think I write fast, but carelessly, but always pretty damn spontaneously, which may be both a strength and a weakness.

BLOOMSBURY: I've heard that you are working on an autobiographical novel. If that is so, is it from any attempt to merge the fiction and non-fiction writing you have done?

ABBEY: No. I've got some stories left and I want to write about one good, fat book and then perhaps I'll resign from my author business and do something different. I want to build a house. A stone house. Maybe an adobe houseboat. Raise my children, blow up something. I don't know.

BLOOMSBURY: Your novels might be seen to suggest that all attempts to make a living in the West are destructive. Are there ways to live here that don't destroy the land or humanity of the people?

ABBEY: I believe that farming, ranching, mining, logging are all legitimate, honorable, useful and necessary enterprises. I respect and admire those who carry on these occupations. Especially those who do it in a way that treats the earth with love, and the rights of our posterity with respect. The problem, where things go wrong, is in scale, size, number. The carnage that we're doing to the American West, the planet as a whole, results, I think, mainly from too many people demanding more from the land than the land can sustain.

BLOOMSBURY: In *Good News* a minor character, Glenn, is a piano player who attempts to return to being a composer, a musician, even though he has no audience. Could he be seen as a metaphor for the role of the artist in the West?

ABBEY: No. I don't think so. That character is just being true to his way of life. He will go on making music even for an audience of one—himself. I don't think he's a metaphor for anything more.

BLOOMSBURY: Another character, Sam Banyaca, is a Zuni who presents himself as a magician, able only to do sleight of hand, yet at several key points in the novel, he performs with the real power of a shaman. Are you presenting Indian traditions of mystic power as viable for non–Indians in the modern, technological world?

ABBEY: I'd rather not explain that. There is an explanation for it in the novel that is bigger than you suggest, but I don't want to try to explain it. Yes, I do think Indian beliefs, traditions, and customs have much to teach us. We have much to learn.

BLOOMSBURY: Is there a difference between Sam and, say, Carlos Castaneda?

ABBEY: I've said all I want to say about Castaneda. Sam is a trickster and occupies a special position. There is a narrow line between magic tricks and power. A difference that won't quite fit in words.

BLOOMSBURY: Do you consider yourself a practical man or a romantic man?

ABBEY: I'm a practical romantic. I worry about making a living, raising my three children, getting my wife through college, paying my bills. I've got myself trapped in the same sort of mortgage situation as most other people around. But I have to make a living one way or the other. To that extent I'm a practical man.

BLOOMSBURY: To what extent are you a romantic?

ABBEY: Well, I love to be in love . . . with many things. I tell you, these are rather probing questions you're getting at here.

That's an interesting question, though. I do consider myself a romantic. Partially, I suppose, because I'm an idealist. I still think it's possible to find some better way to live, both as an individual and as a society.

And I have the usual romantic ills—thinking things must be more beautiful beyond the next range of hills. I've been fascinated by the mysterious and unknown. Those are romantic traits.

BLOOMSBURY: What is the worst possible future you see for the American West?

ABBEY: The worst possible future for the American West is already here. At least I hope it is the worst. I am an optimist. I believe that the industrial, military state will eventually collapse or destroy itself.

The horned toads, the hawks, and the coyotes and the rattlesnakes and other innocent creatures I hope will survive and carry on, and yes, probably a few humans with them, or at least I hope so. I think the human race will get one more chance. I'm not sure we deserve it, but I hope we get it anyway.

I look forward to the day when gasoline becomes so expensive and motor vehicles become so expensive that we all have to go back to horses and walking. I'm willing to give up my truck . . . if everybody else does. All right. Enough of that. You want to go for a walk?

Down the River with Edward Abbey

Tucson
May, 1984

Dear Ed,

The notion of writing *about* somebody I know and like makes me feel gossipy, and a little silly. So I'm writing *to* you and if anybody else wants to look over my shoulder while I do, that's all right with me. Even you can—if you want.

Just before beginning this piece, I reviewed the last, post-humously published book of a writer I often admire, the Argentine Julio Cortázar. The book is called *A Certain Lucas*, and in it there's this passage, which left me puzzled:

> A landscape, a stroll through the woods, a dousing in a waterfall, a road between two cliffs, can only raise up to aesthetic heights if we have the assurance of a return home or to the hotel, the lustral shower, dinner and wine, the talk over coffee and dessert, a book or some papers, the eroticism that sums everything up and starts it up again. I don't trust admirers of nature who every so often get out of the car to look at the

view and take five or six leaps out onto the rocks; as for the others, those lifetime Boy Scouts who are accustomed to wandering about covered by enormous knapsacks and wild beards, their reactions are mostly monosyllabic or exclamatory; everything seems to consist of standing time and time again looking at a hill or a sunset, which are the most recurrent things imaginable.

Civilized people are lying when they fall into bucolic rapture; if they miss their Scotch on the rocks at seven thirty in the evening, they'll curse the minute they left home to come and endure gnats, sunburn, and thorns; as for those closest to nature, they're as stupid as it is. A book, a play, a sonata, don't need any return or shower; that's where we reach the greatest heights, where we are the most we can be. What the intellectual or the artist who takes refuge in the countryside is looking for is tranquility, fresh lettuce, and oxygenated air; with nature surrounding him on all sides, he reads or paints in the perfect light of a well-oriented room; if he goes out for a walk or goes to the window to look at the animals or the clouds, it's because he's tired with his work or with his ease. Don't trust, then, the absorbed contemplation of a tulip when the contemplator is an intellectual. What's there is tulip + distraction or tulip + meditation (almost never about the tulip). You will never find a natural scene that can take more than five minutes of determined contemplation, and, on the other hand, you will feel all time abolished in the reading of Theocritus or Keats, especially in the passages where scenes of nature appear.

Perhaps I shouldn't have been puzzled. Cortázar spent most of the last half of his life in Paris, a place that has addled more brains than his. But he wasn't a fool; I'd read enough of his work to know that. And after all, he was an Argentine, a native of a country that has more wildness left in it than even this one does. It couldn't be that he'd never had a chance to see anything beyond Rimbaud's "cold puddle of Europe." Even given the Argentine's most fervent wish to out-Europe Europe in urbanity and "civilization," surely he had read Thoreau, at least—if not Edward Abbey. And where did he think Keats and Theocritus came up with those "passages where scenes of nature appear" in the first place? What was wrong with the man that he could say such patently idiotic things? Or was he saying something I was missing (he did that from time to time)?

Then I re-read *Down the River*, and I realized that he was saying something *he* was missing. I'll explain. In a roundabout way.

In one sense or another, all the essays and articles in *Down the River* are about things of the earth, with a couple of other topics thrown in for the sake of inconsistency (we're on to you, Abbey). Not everything in it was written for inclusion between the covers of a single book: it's a collection of pieces you wrote over several years for a number of publications and reasons. Nonetheless, they're all surges, eddies, waves, rocks in the same stream, all ways of reaching for *la motif*, as your friend Debris calls it in one of the book's essays. And as you say in your introduction, together they have a common purpose (like Cortázar's books, sonatas, and plays, I imagine), "to serve as antidotes to despair."

There's another function the essays serve, too. Like all of your work, like any serious writer's work, they serve to define who you are as a writer and, if John Gardner was right in saying that we are our best selves when we are writing, who you are as a man. If that's presumption, so be it. Gardner was right.

Take the first essay, and one of the best, "Down the River with Henry Thoreau," in which you prove that no matter how many times the blurb-writers call you the Thoreau of the West, you are not Henry Thoreau. You take him with you—or at least his immortal remains in the form of *Walden*—on a trip down Utah's Green River. Sometimes you see through his eyes as you travel, but you also spend a fair amount of time arguing with him, getting peeved with him, occasionally allowing yourself moments of pity for him. What's worth taking from his thought and life, you take. What's worth admiring, you admire. But there's no blind admiration, no mindless aping (as more than a few of this generation have done). He goes with you down the river as a friend you want very much to understand, but also to come to terms with on *your* terms.

You understand, for example, that he found all the adventure he needed in his wanderings around Walden Pond and Concord. But still, no woman, no good beer, no pure love of the impurity of good food? No desire to join George Catlin in touring the great Western plains? Henry lived, you say, "an unnecessarily constrained existence, and not only in the 'generative' region."

He was, in other words, a puritan.

That's not Edward Abbey. Edward Abbey is closer to, say, D. H. Lawrence and his mockery of Ben Franklin's fear of "using venery" than he is to the continent sages of New England—though God only knows how you'll take *that* comparison. I have a notion that Lawrence's sex-sodden philosophies don't excite you much more than Thoreau's puritanism. There's not enough true adventure in either of them. "Though most of my mind and half my heart side with . . . Thoreau," you say in the essay, "Fool's Treasure," "the rest belongs to the imbeciles. I, too, would have gone with the Forty-Niners. Who cares whether we found true gold or only fool's gold? The adventure lies in the search. . . . " The search, the trip down all the rivers of thought and geography chasing the mystery of *la motif.*

And how constrained that makes Julio Cortázar and those like him sound, who prefer only "higher" experience, except perhaps when experience comes to venery. "Our job," you say of yourself and your friend Debris, and I take it you also mean other artists like yourselves, "is to record, each in his own way, this world of light and shadow and time that will never come again exactly as it is today." How sad if that world is limited by urbane and urban puritans to a world of only rooms, streets, raingutters.

You may be a purist—pure water, pure air, pure food, pure honesty—but you'll gladly let the puritans hoist themselves on their own petards, if puritans could bring themselves to eat enough Abbey's Special Pinto Bean Sludge to admit to petarding (petard: from vulg. Sp. *petardo*, "fart," an etymology that I think would please you far more than it would Henry).

And as for finding the abolition of time only in such "civilized" activities as the reading of Keats and Theocritus? You can speak for yourself, Ed. "Each precious moment entails every other. Each sacred place suggests the immanent presence of all places. Each man, each woman, exemplifies all humans. The bright faces of my companions, here, now, on this Río Dolores, this River of Sorrows, somewhere in the melodramatic landscape of southwest Colorado, break my heart—for in their faces, eyes, vivid bodies of action, I see the hope and joy and tragedy of humanity everywhere.

Just as the hermit thrush, singing its threnody back in the piney gloom of the forest, speaks for the lost and voiceless everywhere.

"What am I trying to say? The same as before—everything. Nothing more than that. Everything implied by water, motion, rivers, boats. By the flowing. . . ."

It is the *living* moment which truly abolishes time, that eternal present tense which brings Heraclitus full circle for you. The knowledge that you can't step into the same river twice is far less important than the knowledge that in stepping into one river, you are in a sense stepping into all rivers, with all people, through all time: "What matters is the strange, mysterious, overwhelming truth that *we* are *here now*, in this magnificent place, and never will know why. Or why not."

The participation in the mystery, the partnership of the now. Keats is one key to those. So is the Río Dolores.

Sometimes as I read *Down the River* and others of your books, I find myself fussing with you, gently fussing, as you fussed with Henry Thoreau, for all your admiration of him. (We've fussed face to face about a couple of these things, so I know there's no surprise for you here.) Not because of the contradictions I think you fall into from time to time: only the new puritans who infest us everywhere nowadays would have you, say, turn vegetarian, lie about liking venison (it's the *wanton* killing you hate, as did Thoreau). I've got nothing against mere contradictions: I'm told I've been guilty of one or two myself. Only math texts don't contradict themselves, and nobody ever picked up a math text to learn about life. Do you contradict yourself?—to steal the Whitman line. Then you contradict yourself. You are large. You contain multitudes. As we all do.

No, I fuss with you when you begin to romanticize the past of American Indians too much, for example, in the same book in which you write, in wondering about the lives of people who lived a hundred years ago in a Western mining town: "And where the work was hard, dangerous, the recreation crude and sometimes brutal, we might assume that those who lived here acquired personality traits adapted to their condition: a hardness of spirit, a relative indifference to suffering."

Yes, good point. Probably true.

Yet if it is true, what might we assume about a culture that hung babies from their feet in trees to teach them not to cry, that massacred their enemies in such exquisite ways (I know, I know, so did we), that took human scalps as trophies? To say that the American Indians' was a "bold, brave, heroic way of life, one as fine as anything recorded history has to show us," and let it go at that is a contradiction of a different color. If hard ways of life lead to a hardness of spirit, and a relative indifference to suffering, no race, no culture can be immune.

(As for the comment for which you've already taken enough flack: "The one thing we could do for a country like Mexico, for example, is to stop every illegal immigrant at the border, give him a good rifle and a case of ammunition, and send him home," because the alternative is "leaving our borders open to unlimited immigration until—and it won't take long—the social, political, economic life of the United States is reduced to the level of life in Juarez, Guadalajara, Mexico City, San Salvador, Haiti, India"—I won't add any flack. But give me a choice of living in Newark or Guadalajara, then go hide and watch how long it takes me to make up my mind.)

But when I'm done with my minor fussing, I'm back on the rivers with you, back in the mystery they represent to you. That notion of mystery is something you return to again and again, arguing with Bucky Fuller and Einstein about whether or not the earth and the universe are "comprehensible" in any sensible way. "A life full of wonder—wonderful," is what you're after, and you don't find that in any universe scientifically miniaturized into comprehensibility. "The most mysterious thing about the universe," you say in your superb essay about the windhover, "is not its comprehensibility but the fact that it exists. And the same mystery attaches to everything within it. The world is permeated through and through by mystery. By the incomprehensible. By creatures like you and me and Einstein and the lizards."

You're a watcher of the mystery, then, a watcher and a protector. Is there a better metaphor for what you do than the image of yourself living in a fire tower, doing your "job of watching," as you say in the same essay? "We watched the clouds again and the weather, and approaching and departing storms. We watched the sun go down behind Four Peaks and the Superstition Mountains, that sundown legend retold and recurring every evening, day after day. We saw the planet Venus bright as radium floating close to the shoulder of the new moon. We watched the stars, and meteor showers, and the snaky ripple of cloud-to-cloud lightning coursing across the sky at night. . . ."

"The forest spread below us in summer in seventeen different shades of green. There were yellow pine and piñon pine, blue spruce and Engelmann spruce, white fir and douglas fir, quaking aspen, New Mexican locust, alligator juniper, and four kinds of oak. Along the rimrock of the escarpment, where warm air rose from the canyons beneath,

grew manzanita, agave, sotol, and several species of cactus—
prickly pear, pincushion, fishhook. Far down in the canyons,
where water flowed, though not always on the surface, we
could see sycamore, alder, cottonwood, walnut, hackberry,
wild cherry, and wild grape. And a hundred other kinds of
tree, shrub, and vine that I would probably never learn to
identify by name."

And Cortázar *complains* that a hill or a sunset are "the most
recurrent things imaginable," pronounces ex cathedra that
"you will never find a natural scene that can take more than
five minutes of determined contemplation."

In language neither monosyllabic nor exclamatory, thus,
thus you refute Julio Cortázar.

When you spot a fire, you report it, sometimes (if you can
get to it) try to help put it out, as your political essays in aid
of stopping needless nuclear power plants, dams, and other
such perniciousness on the part of the technocrats, bureau-
crats and the rest of the rats show. That's part of getting
down the river, too.

What counts is that you're a watcher *and* a participant.
You go down into the woods and meet the bears. Philosophy naked always embarrasses you a little, though you can
sit in the temple and argue with the best of them. But you
can seldom allow yourself a flight of thought that you don't
undercut soon after with Abbey wit or the admission of
uncertainty, a "yes, but." (That's all right: Mark Twain
would approve. Puncturing pomposity is an old American
virtue threatened with extinction.) "Though a sucker for
philosophy all of my life," you admit in "Meeting the Bear,"
"I am not a thinker but—a toucher. A *feeler*, groping his
way with the white cane of the senses through the hairy jun-
gle of life. I believe in nothing that I cannot touch, kiss,

embrace—whether a woman, a child, a rock, a tree, a bear, a shaggy dog. The rest is hearsay. If God is not present in this young prickly pear jabbing its spines into my shin, then God will have to get by without my help. I'm sorry but that's the way I feel. The message in the bottle is not for me.''

Which brings us back to Julio Cortázar, a great lover of messages in bottles. It's not that you don't respect those gifts of "civilization" that he so loves. I've seldom known a man with such a profound respect for books and writers as you— except those books and writers you suspect of nonsense, in which case you're murderous, as the reviews in *Down the River* make wickedly clear. No, the great difference in yourself and a man like Cortázar is that you leave room in the civilized universe for Theocritus *and* wild rivers—not to mention wild river rats.

That's what Cortázar is missing in what he's saying: those tacit definitions of his, those unquestioned assumptions. "Civilized people," for example. "Home."

Is Paris all there is to civilization? Is Buenos Aires? New York? Dear Lord, must a man as brilliant as Julio Cortázar blind himself just to prove he can walk with a cane?

"Wilderness complements and completes civilization," you answer. "I might say that the existence of wilderness is also a compliment to civilization. Any society that feels itself too poor to afford the preservation of wilderness is not worthy of the name of civilization." And in another place: "Civilization remains the ideal, an integrated realization of our intellectual, emotional, and physical gifts which humankind as a whole has nowhere yet attained."

Not even in Paris, Ed?

But "civilized people" will "curse the minute they left home to come and endure gnats, sunburn, and thorns," says Cortázar. Will they? Perhaps, if home means only a 2BR,

LR, DR apartment with an as-it-were view, means no more than an easy chair and scotch at seven thirty (surprisingly, scotch and river water at seven thirty *is* considered a possibility by some moderately civilized people). But there is another kind of home to come home to. Here's how you define it: " 'A man whose emotions are alive,' wrote Saul Bellow, 'is at home anywhere.' Now this may be true for an urbanite like Bellow, who has lived his life inside walls and under a roof; big cities, it's true, are pretty much the same everywhere. But a countryman has a place on earth that is his own, and much as he may love to wander, as I myself do, he loves the wandering more because he has a place to return to, a place where he belongs. A place to live and when his time comes, a place to die. The earth has fed me for half a century; I owe the earth a body. The debt shall be paid."

Deserts, mountains, woods, rivers. Places which *are* home to at least one civilized man.

Leaving Cortázar, breaking camp, back on the river. People who don't think much of you tell me there's an Abbey cult out here in the West, a kind of Abbeyanity that would make Aleister Crowley proud. I wouldn't know about that. If there is one, I'm not a member. Like Thoreau, I don't consider myself a member of anything I didn't join, especially cults. I don't think you're a member either.

In fact, very likely the only rivers I'll ever go down with you, Ed, are these magic rivers of your books. (You do believe in magic, both good and bad—and you know the difference between magic and superstition.) In your introduction to *Down the River*, you tell the story of your first attempt to get out onto a river, the time you and your brother launched yourselves off in a heavy cement-mixing box and forthwith sank. Once when I was about the same age as you, I imagine, at the far southern end of those Appalachians into whose northern river you put your first *bateau îvre*, I launched my first one, also home made. The results were the same, and I imagine the impulse was pretty much the same, too. To chase *la motif*, go after the mystery 'round the bend. My grandfather, I'm told, used to take off for weeks at a time and live alone in a cave on an Alabama river called the Black Warrior, eating only the fish he caught and maybe a few biscuits and beans he cooked up. When I was younger and things would get tough, I used to close my eyes and imagine that if things got tough enough, I could always find that cave.

I know now I can't. It's somewhere near the bottom of a generic power-company lake that bears the generic name of Smith. But I'm still stuck there. My own mysteries still live there, in what's left of those slow, green Southern rivers my mother had to row across to get to school, in the stillness of their shadowy sloughs at the foot of those tree-heavy bluffs where I first fell for rivers. I'll never get over that first love, I imagine, a sucker for sentiment to the last. These noisy Western rivers are a little too uppity and quick-tempered for me. I'll stick with the deserts and the mountains and the woods. And, forgive me River Spirits, swimming pools now and again.

But for God's sake don't *you* stop going down your rivers, either physical or metaphysical. I need those trips; *we* need those trips, those of us who must forever be reminded what it's like to "think like a mountain," but "feel like a river," who've become hopelessly addicted to sharing the magic and the madness. Without those healing waters, where else would we come to drink our antidotes to despair?

> *Un abrazo fuerte,*
> Bob

VOLUNTE

Paul Bermeister
Development lab
Development and

5209 Russell Ave NW
#407

Seattle WA 98107

Diane Wakoski

Joining the Visionary "Inhumanists"

I think I could turn and live with animals, they are so
 placid and self-contain'd,
I stand and look at them long and long.

They do not swear and whine about their condition,
They do not lie awake in the dark and weep for their sins,
They do not make me sick discussing their duty to God,
Not one is dissatisfied, not one is demented with the
 mania of owning things,
Not one kneels to another, nor to his kind that lived
 thousands of years ago,
Not one is respectable or unhappy over the whole earth.

(Part 32, "Song of Myself," Walt Whitman)

The term "inhumanist" is one coined by Robinson Jeffers
to mean a person who rejects the philosophical tradition of
the humanists, that tradition created in classical Greece which
has dominated Western civilization, which sees all human
endeavor as the central purpose of life, and in fact sees all
life as having relative (and less) importance to human life

and activity. But just as the American culture has spawned a new poetry, which really sees no need for classical metrical conventions and practices to make verse, it has also spawned a tradition growing out of both scientific awareness and rebellion against European civilization's domination, that says perhaps the human end is not really so important as we think. In Jeffers's poetry, much of it focused on the natural landscape of Carmel and Big Sur in central California, where he lived, the message is not only a cosmic one— the earth but a small part of the universe, and humans such an infinitely small part of the possibilities of life—but also a neo-Darwinian one in which humankind is a sort of evolutionary mistake, having turned into a murdering, raping, torturing, ravaging species which will certainly destroy itself while other life in the universe, perhaps even on the planet, will live on.

Even though the passage quoted above shows that possibility in Whitman, he is for the most part a true humanist who simply chooses to believe that all mankind *could* be filled with love if it would, and that slavery, war and other ignominies will be wiped away when his bigger vision is obtained. Still, all the seeds of "inhumanism" are planted there in that vision, which does see man as pillaging rather than loving, and does idealize animals for at least not having the worst human vices. Jeffers, on the other hand, sees the human drama playing itself out, doomed and fascinating in its fated self-destruction. When Jeffers's editors at Random House in the forties finally realized what he was saying and were confronted by his antiwar politics in very specific terms, lumping Roosevelt, great American hero, along with Hitler and Mussolini, they not only censored some of the poems in *The Double Axe* (containing the long poem with one section entitled "The Inhumanist"), they wrote an editorial note, placed in the front of the book, disclaiming any of the ideas expressed in the book. The fear, not just patriotic or chauvinistic, of expressing a feeling that the human race was not the most important thing we could know, shocked everyone. This was not politics. It was an undermining of civilization.

Racing along under the surface of all of Ed Abbey's writing is that fiery "inhumanist" philosophy. It makes him love the desert above all things, but equally to have a desire to be in the wilderness anywhere, to explore and understand and simply be with the non-man, the a-human world. But pumping just as strong as a heart inside him, is the tradition, his education, and his feeling that we must believe in human civilization, must try to save it, equivocating often to try to understand these contradictory urges in himself. In *Desert Solitaire*, near the end of Abbey's sojourn in Arches National Park as a ranger, on Labor Day weekend, a stranger who signs himself J. Prometheus Birdsong keeps him up all night discussing philosophy and what his real position is *vis à vis* the humanist issue. They decide that his only reason for arguing the humanist position at all is that he is human, and can't quite face the possibility that he is of no importance whatsoever. And in another discussion with this friend and fellow camper, Ralph Newcombe, he decides that he is not an atheist but an "earthiest." "Be true to the earth" is his motto. Yet it is in this struggle with the human need to survive, triumph and continue in society and civilization, along with his feeling that humans are irrelevant to the cosmos that makes Abbey's writing so rich. We are not being palmed off with nature-worship, nor are we being forced to see anything but the reality of 20th century man, who has immense resources and chronically uses them badly. At one point in *Desert Solitaire*, Abbey makes

a distinction between "civilization" and "culture." Even
though most of his examples are frivolous, the distinction
is eminent in the argument for Abbey's aesthetic which I
think is neither Whitman's longing ("I stand and look at
them and long and long") for the world of humankind to
be as free and pure of destructive vices, nor Jeffers' cynical
belief that man is simply a mistake in evolution which the
very process of evolution will soon make right and that war
will simply destroy the planet.

Abbey is ultimately both politician and poet, spending
half of his year in the wilderness, half in civilization, working
for the Park Service and giving little programs of "revolution," as he calls them, by which we could set ourselves back
on a constructive course. At the same time, he sees more
and more the desert as a symbol for some ineffable great-
ness (God?), that it is in man's power to approach, perhaps
contain. He says, "I am convinced now that the desert has
no heart, that it presents a riddle which has no answer, and
that the riddle itself is an illusion created by some limita-
tion or exaggeration of the displaced human consciousness."
And yet apparently for Abbey, the illusion is also that it does
not matter whether one attains the answer, but whether
one is allowed to continue the pursuit for it.

Strangely, Abbey is no prophet of doom. Like the desert,
he seems to offer philosophies which do not bring final
answers but lead one to other questions. The desert which
is his passion is loved because it is one of the last things which
no one could want to own. And even when it is temporar-
ily co-opted for uranium ore or other precious minerals, it
is always soon wasted again and finally left to the Abbeys of
the world, those who do not want to own or exploit but
only to be. He is eloquent on the need for wilderness on
this planet. We need places where no one could choose to

be, but because of that will be underdeveloped and thus be symbols of freedom. "The knowledge that refuge is available, when and if needed, makes the silent inferno of the desert more easily bearable. Mountains complement desert as desert complements city, as wilderness complements and completes civilization.

"A man could be a lover and defender of the wilderness without ever in his lifetime leaving the boundaries of asphalt, powerlines, and right-angled surfaces. We need wilderness whether or not we ever set foot in it. We need a refuge even though we may never need to go there. I may never in my life get to Alaska, for example, but I am grateful that it's there. We need the possibility of escape as surely as we need hope; without it the life of the cities would drive all men into crime or drugs or psychoanalysis."

This vision of Abbey's is often co-opted for trendy and fashionable uses, rather than used salvagingly as it might. For Abbey, like Whitman and Jeffers, is trying to find a way to understand his own humanness and failures while not dooming the entire human race. But the inherent paradox in this is unavoidable. In a rhapsodic passage near the beginning of *Desert Solitaire*, he describes killing a rabbit with a stone, just for the joy of being in the wilderness and being able to do it. Not for meat, and not because he is actually a hunter. He is trying to feel himself a part of the landscape. Yet, earlier that same week he has had the problem of what to do about mice in his trailer. They attract snakes, and he doesn't want to live with rattlesnakes. He doesn't want to kill the mice. He doesn't want either to have to kill the Faded Midget, a little horned rattlesnake which has come to live under the steps. Nature solves the problem for him, in one of the most charming parts of *Desert Solitaire*, when Abbey tells the story of his living with a bull snake for a few weeks, in April when it's still cold. The snake loves the warm trailer and often curls itself around Abbey's waist, inside his shirt. It drives away both the Faded Midget from the doorstep and the mice. But Abbey deliberately sets up his wish not to kill, his humanist self—for the reader; then takes his walk into the desert where he savagely kills the rabbit for no reason at all:

> For a moment I am shocked at my deed; I stare at the quiet rabbit, his glazed eyes, his blood drying in the dust. Something vital is lacking. But shock is succeeded by a mild elation. Leaving my victim to the vultures and maggots, who will appreciate him more than I could—the flesh is probably infected with tularemia—I continue my walk with a new, augmented cheerfulness which is hard to understand but is unmistakable. What the rabbit has lost in energy and spirit seems added, by processes too subtle to fathom, to my own soul. I try but cannot feel any sense of guilt. I examine my soul: white as snow. Check my hands: not a trace of blood. No longer do I feel so isolated from the sparse and furtive life around me, a stranger from another world. I have entered into this one. We are kindred all of us, killer and victim, predator and prey, me and the sly coyote, the soaring buzzard, the elegant gopher snake, the trembling cottontail, the foul worms that feed on our entrails, all of them, all of us. Long live diversity, long live the earth!

What finally, then, is Abbey's vision?

Yes, we can say the Dionysian, in which we understand all of life to be part of a cycle, death as much a part of reality as birth, and death required before rebirth can occur. But why then the tirades against "culture" rather than "civilization," the anger against the motor vehicle, his hatred of all the tourists who come to the park? This seems to be different from Jeffers's "inhumanism" when looked at entirely; there is no real conviction here that all humanity is a mistake. If there is any political message constantly in Abbey's writings, it seems to be that we have overpopulated the world. Not that mankind is bad. Only that certain humans are, and that in large numbers humankind is trouble.

Is it specious to conclude that Abbey, like his Desert, presents riddles which have no answers? Perhaps. Yet maybe that is part of the appeal of his work in this time when we are aware of a very probably approaching nuclear holocaust. Perhaps his lack of doctrine or dogma is reassuring in itself:

> The desert says nothing. Completely passive, acted upon but never acting, the desert lies there like the bare skeleton of Being, spare, sparse, austere, utterly worthless, inviting not love but contemplation. In its simplicity and order it suggests the classical, except that the desert is a realm beyond the human and in the classical view only the human is regarded as significant or even recognized as real.

This meditative line, even though not the same as Jeffers's conclusions, is an "inhumanist" speculation. Certainly, it is what is beyond the human in the desert and wilderness which draws Abbey. And all of his readers must thank him, as we thank Whitman and Jeffers, for giving us some respite from our own resolutely self-centered, and probably destructive, humanism.

James Hepworth et al.

Literature of the Southwest Interview

In January 1981 Edward Abbey became a lecturer in the University of Arizona's English Department, employed part time to teach creative non-fiction writing to both undergraduate and graduate students. The following are transcripts of a February, 1981 interview with Edward Abbey by literature students at the University of Arizona.

QUESTION: You did some time at Yale, didn't you?

EDWARD ABBEY: Two weeks. I went to Yale in the fall of '54. I had academic ambitions then and wanted to be a professor of philosophy. I went to Yale to get a master's degree in philosophy, maybe go on to a doctorate. I wasn't sure, but I got scared out by a course in symbolic logic. It was required, and I found it totally incomprehensible. The only job my wife could get in New Haven was as a waitress at Howard Johnson's, and we both decided we were homesick for the Southwest. And those three reasons combined propelled us to bolt. I quit just in time to get my tuition money back. So I flunked out of Yale.

Q: In Albuquerque you were a graduate?

ABBEY: I did finally get my M.A. in philosophy at the University of New Mexico, after chickening out at Yale. I've often regretted it, but never very much.

Q: You grew up where?

ABBEY: Pennsylvania.

Q: Did you come out west as a child? For example, in *Fire on the Mountain* there is a young man who comes to visit his grandfather.

ABBEY: That's all fiction. I first came to the west when I was 17, hitchhiking around the country, in the summer of '44. I knew I was going to be drafted into the army next year, or else go into prison, so I thought I'd spend my last free summer seeing the country. So I told my parents that I was going to run away from home. My father said that was a good idea. "Here's 25 bucks." So I took off and worked my way around the country. Twenty-five dollars lasted as far as Chicago, after that just odd jobs, hitchhiking. It was easy to get a job in those days with the war on; I stacked wheat in South Dakota, worked on a ranch in Montana for about a week washing dishes. I got enough money to get on to Washington, Oregon, California. I was robbed by my best buddy, a fellow who picked me up a week before. We traveled together, he robbed me, and I had to get another job.

Q: And that's in *Journey Home*. What about the story within the story? Do you remember the story Jack Burns tells Bondi about his experiences rustling grub?

ABBEY: Right. I stole that story from my father. He told me something like that when he had worked in a logging camp in Washington state back in the '20s. I liked it, so I used it. He's been threatening to sue me ever since.

Q: Are you at all worried about your son stealing your material?

ABBEY: No, I copyright everything. I do have a son who wants to be an actor, and a director, and a playwright.

Q: Do you encourage this writing business?

ABBEY: No, I don't encourage it. I would much rather see them go into engineering or business administration, so they can support me in my old age, now rapidly approaching, but now they all want to go their own ways so I have to encourage them. Anyway, the oldest son wants to be an actor, and the next oldest son wants to be a musician, my daughter age 12 plays the piano and wants to be a park ranger. They're all going to hell. Where did I go wrong?

Q: If not from your children, have you derived satisfaction from your writing?

ABBEY: Oh, yes, very much. It's awfully hard work for me getting started right at that first page, whether it's a book or a three-page book review. But once I get started, I generally find it easy to continue. I get enthused, involved.

Q: Where do you prefer to write, in town or in the wilds?

ABBEY: When I feel like writing, I can write anywhere under almost any conditions as long as I have paper, pencil, or pen. I have been spending many of my summers in the last few years working as a fire lookout in the Tonto Forest. And that is a good place to write, to read. Very quiet. If you don't write or read, you go mad.

Q: Initially, did you have trouble getting published?

ABBEY: Oh, not really. I was very lucky in the beginning. The very first novel I wrote was sort of a teenage drama set in a small town in Pennsylvania. I wrote that in my senior year at New Mexico. I entered it into a contest that some New York publisher was holding that year. I did not win first prize, but the publishers said they would publish the book anyway. It's a very poor book, I think.

It's out of print and has been ever since about six months after it was published, fortunately. The same publisher published my second, which was *The Brave Cowboy*. Then I ran into some hard times. I wrote two or three novels after *Cowboy* which were all rejected by dozens of publishers.

Q: Why did the critics ignore *The Brave Cowboy* for so long?

ABBEY: Oh, I don't know. Maybe it's not a very good book. But let's not think about that reason. You've already discussed that, I'm sure.

Q: What were your feelings about its critical rejection?

ABBEY: It was published by a New York publisher, and it got a review in the Sunday *Times Book Review*; most novels did in those days, in the middle 1950s. Otherwise, it was pretty much ignored by the national press, although there were a few reviews in local and western newspapers. I think most book reviewing is done in the east, in New York City, and the New York reviewers and critics tend to ignore books from and about the west. They do not take them seriously. California is a different matter. I don't include that in the west. By west, I mean the southwest, Rocky Mountain west. California writers, of course, have done pretty well. Steinbeck, Stegner.

Q: In a recent interview, you said you had trouble with plotting. I find that hard to accept. Do you really have trouble with plots?

ABBEY: No, I don't know why I said that. I guess I was thinking of that last novel *Good News*, in which I tried to do too many things at once and got too complicated. The characters never did get developed. Except for that one, all the fiction that I have written has a very simple, straightforward approach to plot. The plots usually move in a simple, chronological and linear fashion, the beginning to the middle to the end. Maybe I was thinking that I had never tried to develop a complicated or subtle plot and carry it through well, do it well. My basic ideas are very simple; I am a simple-minded guy.

Q: Are you also an anarchist?

ABBEY: Oh, in the realm of idealism, the ideal realm, yes. No, I am not a practicing anarchist. I am very much a member of our society, willy nilly, like it or not. I don't have much choice. I have to pay taxes, I own property now, I'm putting two kids through college; I'm pretty bogged down in the whole catastrophe, just like everyone else.

Q: Do you have a favorite novel that you wrote?

ABBEY: The next one.

Sam Hamill

Down the River Yin

A gray wind off the Pacific. The dark forests of Puget Sound are full of cedar and spruce and Doug fir. Here, a brief hundred years ago, native peoples carved out sea-going vessels from cedar trees that were saplings when Columbus was begging after boats. In Estonia, "Father Spruce" goes back four thousand years. Doug fir is commercial.

Gray skies the first day of May. Gray seas, gray gulls. But it's not the weather that makes me feel so gray. It's what Kawabata Yasunari called simply, "Beauty and sadness." How they fit together, how they compel. Because I have been rereading Edward Abbey's *Down the River*, I have been remembering rivers—the Colorado River running beside Moab, Utah; the San Juan a little on south; the Novarro River south from Mendocino on the northern California coast where I first lived alone in an old Ford van, camping on "Timber Industry" land until they came in and fenced it all; and other rivers, in Alaska, British Columbia, Washington state, and in Japan.

Thinking of rivers on a gray day on Puget Sound, I remember the closing lines of a poem written by Li Yü nearly a thousand years ago:

if you want to know the sum of human pain,
watch the soft brown river rolling eastward in the
     spring.

Rivers often bring me to the edge of tears. Not just the damming of rivers, not just the foreseeable end to the salmon
runs of these northwestern rivers, but something of the river
itself. It reminds me also of a poem by Bashō:

Not just my human sadness,
hototogisu,
but your solitary cry.

The hototogisu is the Japanese cuckoo. There is a resiliency
in the clear perceptions of Kawabata, Li Yü, and Bashō
that I have always found attractive. I mention this because
these two Japanese and one Chinese gentlemen have been
with me in much the same way that Mr. Abbey claims Thoreau (it's pronounced *thor*-ough, with the accent on the first
syllable):

I carry a worn and greasy paperback copy of a book
called *Walden, or Life in the Woods*. Not for thirty years
have I looked inside this book; now for the first time
since my school days I shall.

Except that my greasy books are dog-eared from use. From
Bashō's journey to the north, as from Tu Fu's, I have learned
much that has shaped my mind and heart.

But Mr. Abbey makes claims for *Walden*'s author that trouble me. "I found that by working six weeks a year I could
meet all the expenses of living," he quotes. Perhaps I am
reading this wrong, but I can't help wondering what our
Victorian amateur naturalist would do with the remaining
46 weeks of the year. And so forth.

Sam Hamill

There are moments in Thoreau's journals when I like him; there are wonderful passages on his Concord and Merrimac travels; but *Walden* is an ugly little book. Let me quote one of our finest literary journalists, Hayden Carruth, on *Walden*:

> That's what *Walden* is: a work conceived in rancor and composed in scorn. It is an elitist manifesto, a cranky, crabby diatribe. Its victims are its readers, and none escapes. Its author was sanctimonious, self-righteous, and ungenerous to the point of cruelty. . . . At one point he tells how, when he was walking along the railway, he saw a large toolbox, and "it suggested to me that every man who was hard pushed might get such a one for a dollar, and, having bored a few auger holes in it, to admit the air at least, get into it when it rained and at night, and hook down the lid, and so have freedom in his love, and in his soul be free." His very words: "freedom in his love"—in a box! So Thoreau solves the problem of sex by masturbation, and the problems of all humanity by isolation.

One cannot but wonder whether Thoreau's box served at some point as inspiration for Samuel Beckett's garbage cans. For Thoreau is a moral cripple. For all the beautiful things he said, for all his proclamations about preferring truth to imagination and so forth, he was a man without compassion. He was also a man who had no woman for a friend. On nearly every page of *Walden* one finds a spiritual violence combined with chaotic declarations of self-esteem. "I'm a *real* humanist," Mr. Abbey asserts, "I'd sooner shoot a man than a snake."

But I've been told again and again that Mr. Abbey's declarations of violent intent aren't meant to be taken literally. But, if that is true, just how *are* we to take them?

The ancient Chinese believed (and I believe) that our essential nature is still. And that compassion is the foundation of wisdom. Kung-fu tse says all wisdom is rooted in learning to call things by the right name. What is missing in *Walden* is sometimes missing in Mr. Abbey's appreciation of that book: restraint. It is too easy to appeal to what is base in human character, to gain popularity by saying what the audience wants to hear. It is too easy to recommend *Walden* without reservation.

Some years back, Gary Snyder told me a story. It seems there was to be an ecology teach-in or some such thing. Mr. Snyder, at his own expense I understand, printed a few hundred copies of an essay he'd written ("Four Changes," if memory serves), and sent them off to the get-together because his own schedule didn't permit his attendance. He sent the essays to Mr. Abbey to pass on to the participants. After no word for some time, Mr. Snyder wrote to ask, "Did you get the essay? Did you pass it out? What did you think?" And the answer came back: "Got the essay. Passed it out. I liked it, except for the Buddhist bullshit."

Hearing this story from a man who has been a devout student of Buddhism for many, many years, it is funny and enlightening. But when Mr. Abbey tells the tale, it begins to have an element of rancor, a smug, self-serving note not at all disharmonious with the tone of *Walden*.

Looking for the stillness at the center of things. And Olson's refrain comes back: I have had to learn the simplest things last. Which made for difficulties.

Calling things by the right names, one's self comes into order. Because one's self is orderly, order comes into the house; because the home is orderly, order comes into the neighborhood; because the community is orderly, order is brought to the state. From the Prince of Heaven down to the commonest of the common, self-discipline is the root.

Mr. Abbey imagines a honeymoon with Henry David married to Emily Dickinson.

She: (raising her pen) Henry, you haven't taken out the garbage.

He: (raising his flute) Take it out yourself.

"If you cannot recognize the order within you, how do you expect to understand the natural order around you?" —Shimaboku Eizo.

Sitting at my desk, looking out at the forest behind the row of houses at this former Army fort, I see a hawk circling, moving slowly and steadily southwest, circling. And I can remember back to the framing of my small house, a few friends dropped by to help. And Ernie Baird would suddenly say quickly, "Hawk!" And we would stop and watch, saying nothing because there was nothing to say, because saying nothing said it all. Silence is, I believe, the highest form of moral superiority. Not in the sense of Mr. Thoreau, but in the sense of meditation, in the way Jesus stood in his silence before asking, "Thou sayest it."

And now the hawk is gone over the trees, over the gray waters of the Pacific northwest, into the darkest corners of the human heart.

And what is left is not even memory, only the vaguest notion of a knowledge that inhabits, perhaps, the gene pool itself—the *feel* of natural order Mr. Abbey has so eloquently articulated in *Desert Solitaire, The Journey Home, Abbey's Road*, and elsewhere.

But in this Taoist-Buddhist-Confucian view of things, where is there room for invective? We have elected a government which, following the wishes of the People, has made us little-loved as we have ever been in this world. And what invective will stand out against Holocaust, against the sound of the MX missile, against the ultimate nuclear nightmare—what name-calling can possibly help us recover from our own suicidal impulse?

In a perversion of Confucian reason, the Pentagon declares that the construction of MX missiles will help business; business, in turn, will require more employees, and all of this will, of course, help to bring the nation into economic equilibrium. Contemplating the 24,000-year half-life of plutonium 239, Mr. Abbey drinks beer. This is invective of the highest order, a gentle nose-thumbing at international stupidity that would earn a small smile from Tu Fu or Kung-fu tse. This is the *wu-wei*, action through non-action. The sort of restraint one admires when one remembers another military headquarters that promised work would make us free.

"He says that woman speaks with nature. That she hears voices from under the earth. That wind blows through her ears and trees whisper to her. That the dead sing through her mouth and the cries of infants are clear to her. But for him this dialogue is over. He says he is not part of this world, that he was set on this world as a stranger. He sets himself apart from woman and nature." This is the opening paragraph of Susan Griffin's *Woman and Nature*. Two hundred pages later, Susan Griffin says, speaking of her sister, Earth: "I do not forget: what she is to me, what I am to her."

And I think: I would like to eavesdrop on a dialogue between Edward Abbey and Susan Griffin.

In Mr. Abbey's books, men are men. They drink beer and float rivers and sweat and piss in parking lots and cuss like a bunch of good old boys on a binge in the desert. I suspect they are a little lonely. Because there aren't many women around.

And I think that most of our men are like that. Because they've alienated themselves from the domicile. A hundred years ago, the home was the major point of manufacture in the civilized as well as primitive world. We have sought *wyfdom* as a form of exploiting indentured servantry. We have forgotten the true meaning of husbandry.

That unpleasant fellow, Henry David, won't take the garbage out. He is miserable and reclusive not because he so loves "nature," but because he is alienated from the essential duties of being alive.

I wonder what kind of *stuff* Mr. Thoreau dumped in that pond.

He'd probably shudder to hear another old geezer in gray whiskers say it, but I love Edward Abbey. He's a high-class quarrel. While every pseudo-eco-freak in the country is toasting tofu, he's off with a beer pissing vinegar into the fuel tank of a D-8 Cat.

He cuts a singular trail, teetering on the brink of hypocrisy. He commits a good-natured heresy.

I'd like to buy him a beer. And ask a few questions about his home. Like who is his wife. How many kids has he had. How many ex-wives. I'd like to talk about population, commitment, balance in personal affairs.

Because I love Edward Abbey, and because I'm a *real* feminist, I'd rather quarrel with him than shoot him.

Because I love Edward Abbey's books, I have committed this heresy, I have raised some issues that have been nagging me through many of his books for many years. I do so because I'm certain that the praise for his achievement will be fulsome. And because I'm sure he won't mind. Except for the Confucian bullshit. And the feminist bullshit. And the Taoist.

And that's fine. Perhaps some day we will meet and share a jug of wine on the banks of the River Yin.

A Letter to Ed Abbey

Dear Ed,

You know, the reason that we never had further correspondence (I guess) was not—as you suggest in the book—because of any comments about Buddhism, but just because it didn't happen. So it does happen that I write you now, though again, curiously enough, on the point of Buddhism. George Sessions forwarded me some of the questions from the letter you wrote him 22:VIII:82 suggesting I might want to deal with them, and I might as well.

The bad rap that has been put on India and Far Eastern cultures, by half-baked historical information, is hard to undo. It's a matter, I suppose, of getting out of Utah or Arizona grooves, as much as us on the coast getting out of "California" grooves. What I have to address first is your statement that these are the "most miserable, most abused, most man-centered cultures on earth." I don't know where you got that notion. India, of course, is a totally different culture, and essentially an occidental culture, as against the Far East. The Himalayas, the drainages of the Irrawaddy, the Sutlej and the impenetrable mountains of Yunnan separate the Far East from India. Also there are the little matters of total racial difference and total linguistic family difference. India has been, it's true, a nation with considerable problems for the last few centuries. Many of these problems were brought about by the deliberate policies of England, who for some decades dumped textiles in India until the local weaving industry collapsed and then sold Manchester goods at an elevated price to a captive consumer audience. There are studies on how Europe impoverished the rest of the world. Just because they are by Marxists, I wouldn't necessarily slight them. Like Mexico by the Spaniards, India was encouraged in many ways to give up its local sustainability. You might know that opium was developed by British industry as a crop in Nepal in the low lying areas, and then to guarantee that there was a market for it, Britain shoved opium down the throats of the Chinese population. This was called the "opium war." China, your purgatory, has not yet forgotten the injustice and indignity of having drug addiction forced on it by the west.

But to go on: India has an average population density of about forty to sixty persons to the square mile, as I recall, which is about that of Hungary or Czechoslovakia. It is not particularly densely populated—especially compared to Belgium, or Java. It had up through the Gupta period one of the most affluent civilizations on earth—a lot of it went down through a combination of goats and deforestation. The goats, of course, eat the reproduction. Soil erosion, deforestation, sheep and goats, as economic devices of agrarian societies are not the invention of Hinduism or Buddhism. From the Neolithic onward, these are domesticates that have been part of agrarian economies everywhere. I dare say you are aware of the fact that Greece and much of Italy once were covered by pine and oak forests, with fine pastures and springs, and the present chaparral brush of most of the Mediterranean in no way represents the plant communities of early historic times. This also was deforestation and goats. We could just as well attribute the deterioration of early civilized environments, then, to democratic Athenian orators, as we could to these sick oriental religions.

The great early Indian king Ashoka was one of the few world leaders, to my knowledge, who actually went so much against the grain of the dynamics of agrarian states as to have carved on rock instructions about not taking the life of animals, and of compassion for non-human beings. The "rock edicts of Ashoka."

Even with the problems that India has had, though, and still has, it strikes me that it's remarkable how hard the villagers try to keep their patience and keep in tune with wild nature. Articles on attacks on villagers by tigers in the Nepal Terai remark on how many months or years it will be that village people tolerate occasional death of one of their members on account of some elderly, ailing tiger, before they finally go to the government hunter for help. Situations where an American or probably European population would immediately form a posse with five hundred .300 rifles and jeeps are totally different. In my own travels in India, as well as studies, I was deeply impressed by the interpenetration of bird and animal species with the agricultural areas. The environmental disruptions of India are probably little worse than those of, say, Italy, Sicily, or much of Greece. The mountains at the headwaters of the Adriatic were once covered with marvelous forests; they disappeared to keep supplying the Roman fleet.

China is much the same case: though forests and soils have suffered greatly in the lower watersheds of the Yangtse and the Yellow, western Chinese mountains and the mountains of northern Siberia are still well-forested. As with India, China was for a spell one of the most splendidly civilized and wealthiest countries on earth. Their cultural high point was probably the 13th century; when they were on the edge of great literacy, inexpensive editions of encyclopedias of all kinds of learning were available to the public, sophisticated instruments such as letters of credit were making the economy seem virtually modern, and a number of Buddhist and philosophical schools enjoyed great debate with each other. The century of violent Mongol rule helped bring an end to all that.

As for Japan, if you have been there, I suspect it has been only to Tokyo and the strip down to Osaka. It is certainly technologically busy, but it is also a culture which still knows how to relax, play, and enjoy great conviviality. Every time I visit Japan, I am struck by how gracefully they deal with their crowdedness, and how well they are able to enjoy life in inexpensive ways. The back-country from the major cities is astonishingly green and natural. Agriculture runs out the shoestring valleys, but climb any Japanese hill and you look out upon mile upon mile of forested mountains. When I was living in Kyoto, the newspaper reported much sighting of bears only twelve miles north of town. A city of three million. The last bear became extinct in England in the thirteenth century. Japan, a country of much larger population and about the same size as England, still has bear, wildcat, foxes, little mountain goats called kamo, deer, monkeys, and a host of other animals from their original days, still not too far off in the woods. The northern island of Hokkaido—which has again an average population of about sixty people per square mile, the same as Czechoslovakia— has an estimated population of three thousand giant brown bears (relatives of the grizzly and the kodiak). Not to mention a huge deer population. The reluctance of Japanese people to go on punitive expeditions against marauding wild pigs, etc., again is a striking contrast to the ways of westerners.

I have tried to describe a little what I think the actual conditions in these countries are. Certainly, human numbers and human greed have done little worse here than they have in other parts of the world: if anything is to blame, it is the nature of that type of social organization we call "civilization" itself—kingship, ruling elites, and the accumulation of wealth. Buddhism (which incidentally does not teach that everything is "illusion" but teaches that the way people see through their self-centered personal interest rosy glasses of subjectivity is "delusive"—and teaches people to see the world "as it is" which is the "real world" rather than the "illusory world" of subjective opinion) has not had a great deal of influence on the civilizations it co-existed with, it's true. Such teachings are never terribly successful on a large scale in any civilization, because they truly run against the grain. Philosophically, early Buddhism is closer to pre-Socratic Greek philosophy than anything else probably. Still, though Buddhism did not make so wonderful an impact, its truth and validity remains and I am grateful for the fact that it tempered medieval north India, Tibet, China, Korea, Japan, Mongolia, Burma and Thailand, in its attitudes at least toward taking life to the extent that people in those realms still are tender-hearted toward birds, animals and trees. There have probably been other worthwhile by-products of the Buddhist presence in the Far East—architecture and art, cooking, manners, poetry and drama, a few little touches. You see, I look on the usefulness of Buddhism as in some ways just beginning now: though its very survival up till now is a marvel. Inside the Zen tradition there has been kept alive a person-to-person mode of actual body-and-mind-training (in the matter of purging one's self of subjectivity) that is extraordinary, in the face of normal history. I won't argue any further as to what I think the virtues of Buddhism might be for the future—a non-anthropocentric species-wide compassion has value of its own.

I don't know what American Zen Buddhist types you have seen. There are all sorts, but if you were to take one example—the San Francisco Zen Center—and its impact on the community, you'd notice that it works in the world with good baking (the bakery); good cooking (the "Greens" restaurant); good sewing (the stitchery); good manners, good donation of good volunteer labor to good projects, a little good art, much good humor, some peace activism via the Buddhist Peace Fellowship, and lots of people who are doing no harm at the very least.

Thinking back on what I've just written, in response to your notions about Asia, I swear it's like you had exactly the same view of Buddhism and China as my Texas Methodist aunt. Stereotypes die hard.

But onward: To comradeship, and the work that must be done. I think a grand mix of environmental religions is just fine, if it does no harm, and I welcome neo-shamanists, mother-goddess worshipers, neo-pagans, and whatever else to the scene if that helps them get the energy to go to work against industrial civilization. Even Marxists! (I forgot to say: I really can't accept China as quite the purgatory you describe it. It was pretty bad through the Cultural Revolution, but they seem to be doing quite well now, with no self-deception—a billion people, and they know they are just barely scrabbling by, trying to make it work. I met with eight writers from the People's Republic three weeks ago in L.A., and was struck by their honesty, humility and sense of the enormity of the task of sheer survival ahead of them. They are serious about birth control.)

So, let's get together under the general name of Deep Ecology and roust out the troops. I loved the *Monkey Wrench Gang*, me and my boy laughed all the way through it. So in the letter I wrote Dave Foreman I was not knocking the *Monkey Wrench Gang* as literature, or theater, or device, but as you know, questioning how we want to handle, seriously, the point of possible violence in the movement. I stand by what I said there—we need warriors, not rhetoricians. And anybody who is truly intent on radical action, doesn't go shooting their mouth off about it, like some of those guys do. But I love their energy and consider myself essentially in the same boat. I hope you consider me in your boat as I consider you in my boat, and hope we can walk some ridge or canyon together somewhere sometime; if you are coming to California let me know and we'll get together up here at my place and get George up here too—

> Fraternally,
> Gary

Bibliography

Books by Edward Abbey

Fiction

Black Sun (1971)
The Brave Cowboy (1960)
Confessions of a Barbarian (1986)
Fire on the Mountain (1962)
The Fool's Progress (1988)
Good News (1980)
Hayduke Lives! (forthcoming, 1991)
Jonathan Troy (1959)
The Monkey Wrench Gang (1975)

Nonfiction

Abbey's Road (1979)
Appalachian Wilderness (with Eliot Porter, 1970)
Beyond the Wall (1984)
Cactus Country (with Ernst Haas, 1973)
Desert Images (with David Muench, 1979)
Desert Solitaire (1968)

Down the River (1982)
The Hidden Canyon (with John Blaustein, 1977)
The Journey Home (1977)
One Life at a Time, Please (1987)
Slickrock (with Philip Hyde, 1971)
Slumgullion Stew (1985); reprinted as *The Best of Edward Abbey* (1987)

Books About Edward Abbey

The only book-length study of Edward Abbey is Ann Ronald's academic dissertation *The New West of Edward Abbey*, published by the University of New Mexico Press in 1982 and reissued by the University of Nevada Press in 1987. Garth McCann's short study *Edward Abbey* (1977) is a booklet in the useful Western Writers Series published by Boise State University.

On Abbey's death, editor Douglas Biggers commissioned a number of reminiscences by the writer's friends for *The Tucson Weekly*, published on 5 April 1989 as a supplement to the newspaper called "A Celebration of the Life and Work of Edward Abbey." A useful and entertaining source of much anecdotal information, the supplement contains contributions by John M. Bancroft, Robert C. Baird, Douglas Biggers, Norah Booth, Richard Byrd, Charles Bowden, Kevin Dahl, Jack W. Dykinga, Dave Foreman, Gerry Glombecki, Fred Griffin, Alan Harrington, Robert Houston, Bill Hoy, Barbara Kingsolver, Michael Lacey, W. David Laird, Jack Loeffler, Barry Lopez, Nancy Mairs, Gregory McNamee, Tom Miller, Suzi and Terrence Moore, Gary Paul Nabhan, John Nichols, Doug Peacock, Brendan Phibbs, Lawrence Clark Powell, R.H. Ring, Gary Snyder, Bill Waller, Peter Warshall, Andrew Weil, and Ann Zwinger.

Bibliography

Thanks to the efforts of Southwestern bookmen Lawrence Clark Powell and W. David Laird, the Special Collections Division of the University of Arizona Library is the best source of information on Abbey's life and work. In it are housed scores of original manuscripts, notebooks, diaries, screenplays, published pieces, photographs, and letters to and from some of the world's most important writers and musicians, not to mention Robert Redford, Gloria Steinem, the IRS, and the FBI. Laird remembers Abbey's asking incredulously whether he thought anyone would really *"use* this stuff." The Abbey archives are among the most frequently consulted in the library.

Notes on the Contributors

CHARMAINE BALIAN is an associate with Carson Productions, Ltd.

WENDELL BERRY is a poet, essayist, farmer, and teacher. Among his many books are *Standing By Words*, *The Unsettling of America*, *The Gift of Good Land*, *The Hidden Wound*, *Home Economics*, *Remembering*, *The Wheel*, *The Wild Birds*, and *A Part*, all available from North Point Press.

WILLIAM EASTLAKE is a novelist. Among his books are *Castle Keep* and *Portrait of the Artist with Twenty-Six Horses*. He lives in Bisbee, Arizona.

SAM HAMILL is a poet, essayist, translator, and publisher. Among his many books are *Fatal Pleasure*, *Facing the Snow*, *The Nootka Rose*, *Triada*, and *At Home in the World*. He lives in Port Townsend, Washington.

JAMES HEPWORTH is a poet and essayist. He lives in Lewiston, Idaho, where he directs Confluence Press.

ROBERT HOUSTON is the author of many novels, among them *The Fourth Codex*, *The Nation Thief*, and *Bisbee '17*. He teaches creative writing at the University of Arizona.

ROB LEVIN lives in Atlanta, Georgia, where he works as a freelance journalist for a number of newspapers and magazines.

BARRY LOPEZ is one of America's most respected writers of natural history. His *Arctic Dreams* won the National Book Award for 1986. Among his other books are *Crossing Open Ground; Of Wolves and Men; Giving Birth to Thunder, Sleeping with His Daughter; River Notes, Desert Notes;* and *Winter Count.* He lives in the Cascade Mountains of Oregon.

NANCY MAIRS is a poet and essayist. Her books are *In All the Rooms of the Yellow House, Plaintext,* and *Remembering the Bone House.* She lives in Tucson, Arizona.

GREGORY MCNAMEE is an editor and writer who lives in Tucson, Arizona. He has published a verse translation of Sophokles's tragedy *Philoktetes* and a collection of literary interviews, *Living in Words,* and is the author of a collection of essays, *The Return of Richard Nixon* (Harbinger House).

DAVID REMLEY is professor emeritus of English at the University of New Mexico.

RICHARD SHELTON is a poet and essayist. Among his many books are *The Bus to Veracruz* and *Selected Poems.* He teaches creative writing at the University of Arizona in Tucson.

GARY SNYDER is one of the best-known poets of our time. Among his many books are *Turtle Island, Earth House Hold, Ax Handles, Riprap,* and *The Old Ways.* He lives in the Sierra Nevada of northern California.

DAVID SOLHEIM teaches English at Dickinson State College, North Dakota.

DIANE WAKOSKI has published many collections of poems and is the winner of the 1989 William Carlos Williams poetry prize. She is writer in residence at Michigan State University.